To Tanya
& her mom
all best on your
journey

Missing Links

Vincent Bugy

MISSING LINKS

The True Story of an Adoptee's Search for His Birth Parents

by Vincent J. Begley

CLAYCOMB PRESS, INC.
Chevy Chase

Distributed by
ACROPOLIS BOOKS LTD.
Washington, D.C.

Published in the United States by
Claycomb Press, Inc.
P.O. Box 70822
Chevy Chase, Maryland 20813-0822

Manufactured in the United States of America
10 9 8 7 6 5 4 3 2 1
First Edition

ISBN   0-933905-17-3 cloth
           0-933905-06-8 paper

A Page of Thanks

SINCERE AND WARM thanks to all those who played a part in *Missing Links*. To my wife, Patty, and our children, Jennifer, Jeremy, Nicholas, and Kieran. To my father. To my sister, Patti. To "Aunt Joan" and all the other members of her family. To Tom and his wife Barbara. And of course, special loving thanks to my birth mother.

I would also like to acknowledge the kindness of Mary Claycomb who saw the value in my search. And I would be remiss not to thank Darla Garey-Sage, Joshua M. Levine, and "Margaret" for playing an important part in bringing my story to print.

To Tom and Chase Layman my deep gratitude for their participation in the publication of my book.

Contents

Author's Note

TO PROTECT THE privacy of the families I found in my search and those others who helped me, all names have been changed except those of my wife and children, my adoptive parents, and my sister.

Missing Links

PART ONE

Seek

I am a poet, a seeker,
and a confessor, obligated
to truth and sincerity.

I have a charge,
albeit small and confined:
to help other seekers
to understand and cope
with the world,
if only by assuring them
that they are not
alone.

Hermann Hesse, 1950

PROLOGUE

Great Expectations

TRAFFIC WAS VIRTUALLY at a standstill on 395. Cars were inching their way toward the exit for Washington's National Airport. I thought I had allowed myself plenty of time for the trip from Fredericksburg to the airport, which shouldn't have taken more than an hour and a half, door to door.

That much time had already elapsed when I finally made the turn off the highway to the airport. I still had to park my car, catch the shuttle bus to the terminal, and then find the right arrival gate. I could only hope the flight would be late. With my luck, though, the plane had probably arrived early. I would probably be late.

Damn traffic. Why did I always run into congested highways when I needed to be somewhere on time? Why couldn't it be an uneventful trip? Why was I beginning to feel tense and nervous? My palms were getting wet. My heart was beating faster.

I looked at my watch after I parked my car. "Good," I said aloud. "I still have enough time to get there."

Or so I thought, until I found myself waiting for a shuttle bus to come by and pick me up. I began pacing, looking down the road for any sign of a shuttle bus.

Nothing in sight.

Another glance at my watch.

Damn. Damn. Damn.

What was it about me? Why was I allowing myself to come unglued? There was no reason for it. I'd get there when I'd get there. I had no control over the traffic. And as for the shuttle bus, there was bound to be one here sooner or later. So what was the big deal?

I talked myself out of a minor nervous breakdown, admitting I was sometimes my own worst enemy. A few deep breaths and I was as good as new. I even began to laugh at how foolish it was to get so intense about such trivial matters.

It wasn't as if I hadn't tried to be punctual. I had tried all I could to get to the airport on time. There was no need to punish myself and get all worked up about something that would soon be a thing of the past.

Hadn't I learned from years of experience that things always seemed to go more smoothly when I took them in stride? Wasn't it true that whenever I started to allow the situation to control me, I made one mistake after another? I agreed with myself. And just as I did, I saw the shuttle bus making a turn in my direction.

One more check of my watch.

If the bus made good time, I'd be at the terminal with seconds to spare. If not . . . well, I'd worry about that when the time came. Which it didn't, because the bus pulled up in front of the terminal moments before the plane was supposed to arrive.

One look at the arrival screen had me laughing. The flight I had come to meet was late, about one half-hour late.

"Wouldn't you know," I said, "wouldn't you

know!''

Now I'd have to wait. Waiting had become a persistent pastime. If I wasn't rushing, I was waiting.

This time, however, I was glad for the wait. I needed to collect my thoughts, because this was no ordinary run to the airport to meet and greet a familiar face. I had taken the day off from work to come to National Airport to pick up a stranger. My mother. Or, to be more exact, my birth mother.

This unique day should have been charged with excitement and filled with high drama. How many times does an individual get to meet his birth mother for the first time? Shouldn't such an event be cause for something extraordinary?

I thought of all those times I had read articles about reunions between birth parents and their children. Just reading those articles had moved me. And here I was about to experience such an event—firsthand.

If I was supposed to feel so high, why was I so distracted? If this moment soon to arrive was the culmination of a long-cherished dream, why was I so removed from the situation?

I knew how I wanted it to happen. I knew if I were to write and produce the dramatic scene of first meeting my birth mother, it would be an Oscar-winning sequence. There would be bright lights, technicolor cameras, and momentous action on the set.

There would be a long shot of the terminal to set the mood, with people rushing back and forth, and only one person standing still at Gate 48, waiting for the flight to arrive.

She'd be the first one to get off the plane. The camera would zoom in on her anxious face as she looked at the crowd, hoping to see that one special person waiting for her.

The music would start. Violins and cellos, and then the notes of a flute as her eyes caught those of her long-lost son. The two would move toward each other, every step slowed by the camera. She would hold out her arms to him. He would hold out his arms to her. The music would build as they embraced.

"Hello, Son."

"Hello, Mother."

Cut! Clear the set. Bring back reality.

There weren't any lights or cameras. The only music was the annoying sound of static from the airport's loudspeakers. This momentous event was going to happen sans the Hollywood glitter. Whatever drama there was to be would be the drama of real life. Although I longed for the moment to have some magic in it, I realized the magic would be internal and private, not external and public.

Meeting my birth mother was a branching into a new road that turned off another much longer highway. Where the new road would lead was something I couldn't yet answer. I'm not a fortune-teller; I don't have clairvoyant abilities.

It was just another step, albeit a big step for me, and one that is the dream and nightmare of almost all adoptees. It would bring together the missing links.

Was I prepared to take this step? I wasn't sure. There was some voice inside me that whispered, "Go while the going is good," and another voice urging me, "Stay, it's what you've been waiting for."

Seconds before I realized the plane had landed, I started to panic. Not a wild panic, but the inner panic that comes when childhood butterflies reappear for a command performance. There was no turning back. I was committed to follow through, no matter what was in store.

I looked out the window and saw the plane as it pulled up to the gate. The bright April sun caught the metal of the wing. For an instant, I was blinded by the light.

When the plane came to a stop, I saw its silver body against the blue sky. It was a picture-perfect scene, far different from the scene of my first cautious move toward my search for my missing links. I had taken that very first step only five months earlier, on a night that was as dark as this day was light.

What a difference! What a stark contrast in mood and tone! Here I was at an airport, waiting for my birth mother, when five months ago I had been waiting on a street corner for the light to change to green.

That was the night that made all the difference in the world. I'll never forget it.

CHAPTER ONE

It Was a Dark and Stormy Night

AND BITTER COLD, too. It was the perfect night for solving an English mystery. There was a freezing rain sweeping along New York's Eighth Avenue. People were rushing to get in out of the rain. Too few taxis were being hailed by too many people. Buses and cars were moving along at a snail's pace. Angry drivers were relentlessly blowing their car horns, as if that would somehow miraculously unclog the congestion.

There was no sane reason in the world why I was standing on the corner of 50th Street and Eighth Avenue. I had enough sense to know when to get in out of the rain, but there I stood anyway, a candidate for pneumonia.

I was in New York on business. My day's work was completed, and I was only a block from my hotel, where, instead of standing out in the downpour, I could have been in my room reading a good book or getting ready to go to the theater. That would have been the sensible thing to do. But no, there I was, perched on a windswept corner, watching the light turn from green to red and back, over and over again, until I could predict the exact second when the light would change.

I was locked into dead center, as if caught in some invisible magnetic field that held me prisoner between two equally powerful poles. At the one pole stood tradition and the world as I knew it—that strong force that had always held me back. But the other pole, equally strong, pulled me toward adventure in an unknown world.

Although I was leaning toward tradition, my desire to sally forth in the spirit of Don Quixote seemed, on that night, to be growing in intensity. As the light changed again, I found myself making an unconscious decision in favor of the unknown. With an underwhelming amount of determination, I put my foot forward, sinking ankle-deep into an infamous New York City pothole filled with icy water. At the same moment, a gust of wind came along, rendering my umbrella useless against the rain and blowing my cap down the street.

Why was I willing to fight the elements when it was obvious I was losing the battle? Where could I possibly be going that I couldn't wait until the weather was more favorable?

I was going back to the scene of the crime, or to be more genteel and specific, I was going back to the place where life—as I knew it—had begun. I was going to St. Clare's Hospital where, on July 11, 1948, I had made my world premiere as Edward Joseph Donahue.

Aside from the name I had been given at birth, and my birth date and place, I knew absolutely nothing else. And even what I knew was more accidental than given.

I first learned my birth name when I was about ten or eleven years old. I had gone to the bank with my father who had to check something in his safety deposit box. While he was leafing through some papers, my eye caught a certain blue document that had two names on it: my adoptive name and the name I had been given at birth.

Learning my original name was probably, at that point in my life at least, being given possession of the single most revealing fact about my past. It was the first tangible proof of who I had been. Shakespeare's Romeo might have mused about the insignificance of a name, but to me my birth name meant everything. I can't remember if I'd ever before thought I had an original name, but I know that learning that name was a turning point in my young life.

I had some doubts about my birth date. I wasn't a suspicious person, but I had heard that many adoptees couldn't be certain whether or not their original date of birth was in fact accurate. Therefore, I hesitated to accept my birth date as gospel.

Was that, then, the reason why I was going to St. Clare's? To verify my date of birth? Not really. I was going to St. Clare's to see if there was anything "real" I could learn about who I was and who was "responsible" for my birth.

In truth, I had nowhere else to turn. It would have taken legal action to get access to my court-filed adoption papers. And to get legal action, I would have had to show "just cause" why I should be allowed to see those documents. Since my life didn't hang in the balance, and there wasn't any life-threatening event that could have been eased by gaining access to my adoption file, I didn't have a legal leg to stand on.

Was there anywhere else I could turn? My parents, perhaps? That would have been the most convenient, least disruptive way to search; however, they knew no more than I did.

The only other source of information would have been the New York Foundling Home, where I had been placed after birth. I knew that they knew something at the Foundling, but they weren't going to tell me anything. Or at least, they weren't going to tell me anything of consequence.

How did I know? I had already gone that route. My sister Patti, who was also adopted, and coincidentally, born on July 11 two years before me, had written to the Foundling for some background information. One of her children had been blacking out. Her doctor thought it was probably a genetic condition. Although Patti and her eldest child both experience migraine headaches, blacking out or epilepsy, on the other hand, is thought to represent a diametrically opposed condition that may somehow be physiologically connected to migraine. As an adoptee, my sister couldn't tell the doctor anything about her family medical history.

Although Patti's doctor thought she could learn something about that history by writing to the Foundling, when she did write, she discovered that an adoptee could ask the Foundling to provide any non-identifying background information and would receive that data if it were available. But that was all. By non-identifying, the Foundling meant census information only—dates, birth parents' ages, nationality, religion, and the like. They would not release anything relating to the identity of the birth parents.

Although I had been more interested in learning about the nature and character of my birth parents, I had decided that any information was better than none at all. So I had contacted the Foundling.

What I had learned from their records was less

than earth-shattering. In fact, what they told me confused me more than it settled any doubts I might have had about my origins.

In answer to my inquiries, I had received a letter:

Dear Mr. Begley:

I have read through your records and I regret to inform you that there is very little information in your record. Your date of birth is listed as July 11, 1948 and you were placed in a temporary foster home on October 1, 1948. There is no indication as to where you were during the lapse of three months. You were sickly in the beginning, having a slight rash, ear infection and seborrhea of the scalp. It is possible you were in the hospital during this time.

As you got better, adoption was recommended, and you were placed in the home of Mr. and Mrs. Begley on February 3, 1949.

The only information on your parents is that they were not married. Your father was 34, and your mother was Roman Catholic. There is no information regarding nationality, siblings or grandparents.

I regret that there is no further information I can give you.

Sincerely,

The signature of a Foundling administrator followed.

I remember how baffled I was by the letter. Instead of filling in some of the tiny voids, it created chasms of curiosity. I could easily live without knowing my parents' national origins. Not knowing whether I was Irish, German, or English never really bothered me, probably because my parents never showed much interest in their heritage. If they had, I might have developed a stronger sense of ethnic identity. Not that I think heritage is unimportant. In fact, I think it is *very* important, up to a point: if where one comes from or where one's ancestors once lived becomes more important than one's own identity or that of one's ancestors, then ethnic ties begin to bind. It's admirable to be proud that your grandparents hailed from Italy or Poland, but when people begin to argue that one nationality is better than another, national origins are trivialized. That's why I didn't lose sleep over my unknown national origins. It didn't even interest me much to learn that my mother was Roman Catholic. It only mattered that I was raised in a religious tradition that had provided me with a sense of my own faith.

What bothered me about the letter from the Foundling was what was missing and what was seemingly regarded as insignificant. I had always known when my parents had adopted me. What I didn't know was where I was prior to my adoption. And that was something I wanted to know. Instead of putting that issue to rest, the letter only made the matter worse.

I could live with the fact that I was in a foster home between October 1 and February 3 when I was adopted. But what about the lapse of three months? To tell me "there is no indication as to where you were during the lapse of three months" was ridiculous. A misplaced bootee, no mention of when I might have cut my first tooth, no record of when I started sleeping through the night are the kinds of things I can forgive any institution. But not knowing or revealing where I was for three months? Sloppy record keeping? I doubt it. No organization that has been charged with the care of infants could be so lax as to neglect to record the comings and goings of babies in its charge.

The absence of information about where I might have been during those three months set me to wondering. The only logical conclusion I could come up with was that I might have been placed for adoption right after I was born, but for some reason the adoption didn't work out. Perhaps the fact that I was this scaly kid with a rash all over my body, not to mention an ear infection, was reason enough for some couple to return me to the Foundling before my warranty ran out. Such things did happen to adoptees. Why couldn't I have been returned to the store?

I remember a story my mother once told me. It seems that after she and my father had adopted my sister, they had been invited back to the Foundling for a Christmas party. One of the nuns at the party knew my parents were awaiting word on a second adoption. The nun approached them and asked my mother to follow her up to the nursery where she pointed out a baby boy in one of the cribs.

"That baby," the nun told my mother, "is available for adoption." She turned to my mother, waiting for a reaction. My mother told me that there was something wrong with the baby. She didn't know what it was, but there was something about the baby that just wasn't right.

With the nun patiently waiting for some response, my mother didn't know what to say. She felt that if she declined to adopt that particular baby, she might eliminate all chance of adopting another child. If she agreed to adopt that child, however, she knew she would be making a mistake. She finally told the nun that she didn't think the baby was right for her.

"I understand," the nun said. "We'll just have to wait for the right baby to become available."

That incident happened the Christmas of 1948. I became available less than two months later. If I had

been in a foster home since the previous October, as the letter from the Foundling indicated, why wasn't I considered available? I always wondered what happened between that Christmas party and February 3, 1949, the day my parents got the call that their baby was ready.

It all seemed too odd and clandestine to me, especially considering the fact that my mother didn't get the chance she had been given that night at the Foundling party, to choose or reject me. As she told it, she was cleaning the livingroom in her Brooklyn home, when she got a call from a social worker at the Foundling telling her that a baby was ready that day. She was asked to come over to Manhattan to pick up the baby. My mother said she went into a state of minor panic. There she was in Brooklyn, and my father was at work in Penn Station in Manhattan.

She phoned him to tell him about the call. He told her to get over to the Foundling as soon as she could and he'd meet her there. They arrived in the late afternoon. The nun in charge greeted them and had them fill out the necessary papers. No sooner had they finished signing on the last dotted line, than my mother turned around and saw one of the nurses bringing the baby— me—over to her. If that can't be considered a take-it-or-leave-it situation, I don't know how else to describe it.

I was placed in my mother's arms, and the next thing she knew, she and my father were in a cab taking me to my new home in Flatbush. A strange turn of events, if you ask me.

How did anyone know I was "right" for my new parents? What formula did the Foundling use to determine what baby gets adopted by what couple? And if they did use a formula, what right did they have to develop such a formula for adoption?

Those were just some of the questions I had always had. Add to those the new questions raised by the obscure letter I'd received from the Foundling, and my perching on that street corner waiting to venture forth to St. Clare's becomes more understandable.

Why did I make the decision on that particular night, though, to go seeking information at St. Clare's? The answer is a resounding, ''I don't know.'' I don't know why I happened to pick that night over any other night. I only know that my path would eventually have led to the steps of St. Clare's. If not that cold and rainy night, then on a hot and sunny day in August, or on a breezy day in October. And if not in 1980, then in 1981 or 1982.

Why? Because I had to put some of the missing links together once and for all, not because I was obsessed or consumed by an overpowering need to know why. I wanted to know, because I felt I had a right to know. A right to know about my origins. A right that belonged to me and nobody else. A right that was the birthright of all people. A right that I had been deprived of because I happened to have been an adoptee.

And if I couldn't learn anything more than what my parents knew and what the Foundling told me? Would my life be over?

No. There was far more to my life than adoption. I was my own person. Whatever information I lacked, whatever information I might eventually gain from my search, would not make me more of a person. But it would give me a new dimension. It would bring me to a new level of awareness.

My adoption search was just another step in my

growth. It was not the final step. Whether I came away from St. Clare's wiser for my search or empty-handed, my life was still going to move forward.

The fear I was experiencing that dark and stormy night was both the fear of the unknown and the fear that comes from social conditioning. I had been conditioned as an adoptee in the way only an adoptee can be conditioned. It is a conditioning based more on myth and hearsay than on anything concrete. There had been a certain unwritten, unspoken code of ethics that I, as an adoptee, had come to learn. It was a code that, simply stated, said any adoptee who searched was being disloyal to his or her adoptive parents.

I never wanted to be disloyal to my parents. I never wanted to do anything to hurt them in any way. And although I believed I had a right to know some of the basic things about my life, I was wary of doing anything that could possibly come back to haunt me, and hurt my parents.

My fear was magnified because I was planning to take that first big step without my parents' blessing.

I told myself that I hadn't said anything to my parents, because I had known all along that I wasn't going to find any information at St. Clare's. I told myself that without really believing it. The truth was, I was afraid.

So instead of confiding in them, I had decided to take that first step and see what might come of it. If nothing happened, then it would have been unnecessary to make an issue of my search. And if I did stumble across any relevant information, well, then I would have to re-evaluate my search in terms of my parents. But all that was in the speculative future. I was dealing with reality. And if I didn't want to get run down by a taxi, I would have to get to the other side of the street.

I was undaunted as I headed toward St. Clare's and began to climb the stairs to the main entrance. I suddenly found myself daunted, however, when I noticed the condition of the stairs. They were all cracked and broken. Not quite the steps I expected for the main entrance of a big city hospital.

If the condition of the stairs wasn't enough to cause me concern, I was dumbfounded when I reached the entrance at the top to discover that the doors had been boarded up with sheets of plywood covered with New York's own brand of graffiti. There wasn't a single light on in the hospital. Not a single sign of life.

"Impossible," I said out loud. "Why would anyone board up the doors of a hospital?"

There had to be something wrong somewhere. Hadn't I seen an ambulance from St. Clare's race past me earlier that same day? Surely it would do no good to have an ambulance in operation for a hospital that wasn't open? I stood there at the top of the steps wondering what to do next. Should I call off the search or pursue my folly to the next step? And what was that next step if St. Clare's had been shut down?

I could find out what had happened to the documents that had once been stored at St. Clare's, because there was no way that all the files from a hospital would have been destroyed, even if the hospital had closed. They must have been put in storage somewhere.

Of course. That was my next course of action. I would find out where those documents had been stored and continue my futile search in earnest. I crossed the street to a pay phone and dialed Directory Assistance. I asked for the number of St. Clare's, fully expecting to be told that the hospital was no longer in operation, but that information regarding files could be obtained by dialing . . . When the operator quickly came back with a number for the hospital and not a single word about its being closed, I was surprised. I was even more surprised when I dialed the number and was greeted by a friendly voice announcing, "Good evening, St. Clare's. May I help you?"

I looked over at the darkened hospital and wondered what they had to pay a switchboard operator to work in an abandoned building. When the operator repeated her question, I asked her if the hospital was still open. She must have thought I was crazy, but instead of putting my call through to the psychiatric ward, she politely told me that the hospital was in fact open. When I asked her where the hospital was located, she answered my question without surprise. I thanked her for her help, hung up the receiver, and looked over at the building I had thought was St. Clare's.

I found out later that the building on the corner of Eighth and 50th Street had been a hospital at one time. I had always assumed it was St. Clare's, but in point of fact, it had never been St. Clare's. The real St. Clare's was located two blocks up and two streets over.

My adventure was fast becoming a misadventure. I was not only cold, wet, and tired, but I was also hungry. I should have called off my search for the day, but I was too close to achieving what I had set out to do.

Freezing rain or no freezing rain, I walked the extra distance to St. Clare's and arrived after most of the administrative offices had closed for the day. I went right up to the receptionist and asked her the location of the medical records department. She gave me the floor number without adding that the office had closed, so I took the elevator up to the floor and walked the short distance down the hall to where, to my surprise, I saw an open door.

I could hear a woman talking on the telephone as I entered the office. She didn't hear or see me, because she was sitting behind a glass partition. I didn't want to be rude and interrupt her phone call, but I also didn't want to sit there all night waiting for her to finish her conversation. I cleared my throat casually, hoping that she would hear me. And she did. She stuck her head out from behind the partition and signaled that she'd be with me in a minute.

I had arrived. In a few minutes I was going to learn the secrets stored in the documents at St. Clare's. Or I was going to be politely told that there was no way in hell that I'd ever learn anything from St. Clare's.

I had no idea what I was going to say to the woman in the records department when she got off the phone. I had no speech prepared. I was hoping for divine inspiration.

My blood pressure began to rise as I heard the phone conversation come to an end. I could hear my heart beating as the woman stepped out from behind the glass partition and made her way over to where I was sitting. I tried to look cool, calm, and collected, knowing full well I looked wet, wild, and tired. She smiled at me as she approached, probably sensing that I was terrified.

"My name is Mrs. Chin," she said as she extended her hand. "What can I do for you?"

I expected to blabber, but to my surprise, I almost sounded coherent.

"I was wondering," I began, "how a person would go about getting to see some medical records that might be here at St. Clare's."

Not thinking that was reason enough to see hospital records, I continued talking.

"You see," I told her, "I'm researching a book." That was a lie at the time, because I had no idea that I would ever be writing about my adoption search, but it sounded good, and it was the reason a lot of characters in movies gave when they were in a tough spot.

"Are they your medical records?" she asked.

I told her they were.

Then she asked, "What's your name?"

Oh, God, I thought, here it comes, the name question. How do I get out of this one? If I tell her my name is Vincent Begley, she'll never find anything about me on file at St. Clare's. But if I tell her Edward Donahue, she might ask me for some sort of identification. Then what would I do? I had nothing on me that said I used to be Edward Donahue.

I was in trouble. I had to tell her something. I couldn't just stand there like a dummy. I mean, she asked me a simple question—my name. How difficult should that be to answer? And how long would she wait for my response before thinking I was a lunatic?

I opted to tell her the truth. Or almost the truth.

"Well, Mrs. Chin," I explained, "you see, I was born here at St. Clare's under a different name."

"Oh," she said, as her eyes lit up, understanding my predicament. "You were adopted?"

Bingo! She had said the magic word. Now all I needed was for her to throw me out because by asking to see my original birth records, I had broken some archaic law. Instead of calling for hospital security, Mrs. Chin sat down next to me and began to ask me a few questions. Original name, date of birth, and so forth.

Satisfied that I had given her enough information, Mrs. Chin went on to explain that if my records were still available at St. Clare's, they would have been put on microfilm.

"The microfilm library is downstairs, and they close promptly at five o'clock. If you can come back first thing tomorrow morning, I'll have someone in the microfilm department see if your records can be located."

It was that simple. All I had to do was return to St. Clare's the following day and I would hit pay dirt . . . if . . . If my records were on file. If they hadn't been sealed by the court. If the records for July 1948 hadn't been thrown away because they were too old. So much of my search depended upon a lot of if's. So much of life depends upon a lot of if's.

The odds of ever finding anything at St. Clare's might have been stacked against me, but that didn't seem to dampen my spirits.

When I left the hospital, it had stopped raining and the wind had died down. I returned to my hotel, showered, grabbed something to eat, and then went off to see a Broadway show. I was back in my room a little before eleven o'clock, tired but satisfied. And wondering about tomorrow.

CHAPTER TWO

And What to My Wondering Eyes Did Appear

EXHAUSTION AND ANXIETY are not the two best ingredients for a good night's rest. I must have tossed and turned for hours before I finally fell asleep. My mind was racing at breakneck speed. And if the day's events hadn't given me enough to think about, my evening's visit to see the Broadway production of *Children of a Lesser God* opened up the floodgates.

I had always loved the theater. I wanted to be a part of it. I wanted to see my name in lights on a theater marquee someday. Not as one of the stars, but as the playwright or director. It was my dream. And it was part of a fantasy I had constructed about my origins.

Because St. Clare's had been considered the theater district's hospital I had imagined—or I had wanted to imagine—that I was born there because my birth parents worked in the theater. My birth father was a director. My birth mother was an actress. Sometimes. Other times he was just working behind the scenes and she was just in the chorus. But, whatever role I cast them in, they were theater people because I wanted them to be theater people. It was my way of linking my love of the theater to my birthright. It was a fantasy to dream about.

When my alarm went off a few hours later, neither my flesh nor my spirit was willing to give up the security of my nice, warm, comfortable bed. As I began to drift back to sleep, however, an image of Mrs. Chin telling me I had arrived too late to see my records caused me to bolt out of bed. Although I was only two blocks away from St. Clare's, I didn't want to arrive there a moment too late.

Of course, nothing seemed to go right. I cut myself shaving. I hadn't packed a hairbrush, so I had to do with a little pocket comb to make myself look more like a human being than that specter looking back at me from the mirror.

When it came to packing my belongings, I was all thumbs. It was as if my hands had been injected with a heavy dose of procaine hydrochloride. Everything I picked up seemed to fall out of my hands.

Fortunately, I had allowed myself enough time to have some breakfast in the hotel's coffee shop. I knew if I sat down, had a cup of coffee and something to eat, I'd be able to re-collect my wits. Eating alone has never been one of my pastimes, so I took my breakfast at the counter where I didn't feel so alone because there were people on either side of me. Of course none of us talked. Most people in New York thrive on their privacy, so I didn't expect to engage in animated conversation over my eggs and English muffin, but I could have used some casual chatter at that moment, because I wanted to talk to somebody.

When the two men on either side of me left the counter, I finished the last bit of my muffin and gulped down the rest of my coffee so as not to feel more alone than I already felt.

As I stepped outside onto the street, I was blinded by the brightness of the early morning sun. It was a brisk winter morning, but the sun felt good on my face. I took the bright sun and clear blue sky as positive omens of what might await me at St. Clare's.

When I arrived at Mrs. Chin's office, she was already at her desk talking on the phone. When she saw me, she motioned for me to sit down. I had anticipated another marathon phone conversation, but to my amazement, Mrs. Chin was off the phone in a few short minutes.

"Good morning," she said. "Let's see what we can find out for you."

She removed a piece of paper from her desk before picking up her phone and saying, "Bob, this is Linda Chin. I need you to see if you can locate the medical records of an Edward Donahue. D-O-N-A-H-U-E. Date of birth, July 11, 1948. That's right, Edward Donahue, July 11, 1948. Thanks."

Mrs. Chin hung up and turned to me. "If your records are there, Bob will be able to locate them in a few minutes. He'll call back as soon as he knows something."

I began to wonder what the records—if there were any records—would contain. What clues would they have to help answer the questions of my missing links? Would I be opening Pandora's box, or would I be on the threshold of a wonderful adventure?

The phone rang. Mrs. Chin answered it. She nodded her head as she scribbled something on a piece of paper.

"I see," she said. "Thanks for your help, Bob. Just have somebody bring the microfilm roll up to my office, and I'll see that it's returned to you."

My heart began to race, because it was obvious

from what she was saying that Bob had definitely found something. She placed the receiver in its cradle, looked over at me, smiled, and said, "Bob's located your records." She paused for a minute and then said, "Your mother's name was Maureen."

Maureen. Her name was Maureen.

How odd it was to hear a name attached to a woman who, for years, had only existed in my imagination. My mind began to race ahead of itself. I began to wonder who this Maureen was. Where had she gone? Was she still alive? Had she married? Did she have a family of her own? And what about Mr. Donahue? Who was he? My questions began to overwhelm me. I was getting too far ahead of myself, and that had always been one of my biggest problems. I would begin to create a scenario, and more often than not, the reality of the situation wouldn't meet my expectations.

By the time the microfilm had arrived at Mrs. Chin's office, I was already imagining what it might be like to meet my birth mother. I had to stop thinking what might develop, because I was only setting myself up for some disappointments. I had to take one step at a time.

As Mrs. Chin began to load the microfilm reader, I began to feel a mixture of fear and excitement. Excitement because I always loved a good mystery. Fear because I was the "victim" of this mystery.

Mrs. Chin began to turn the handle on the microfilm reader very carefully. I could see a blur of medical records on the screen. She slowed down until she had located the page that contained my birth records.

When she had focused on the page, she stepped away from the machine. There, for the first time, I saw proof of who I was.

The first thing I learned was my middle name. I had always assumed it was Joseph, because I had noticed the letters Jos. on the adoption papers I had seen at the bank with my father. I had been wrong in my assumption, however. The letters weren't Jos. but rather Jas. for James. I had been born Edward James Donahue, not Edward Joseph Donahue.

The second thing I noticed was my date of birth. There was no longer any question about it. I had been born on July 11, 1948 at 5:48 a.m. to Maureen and George Donahue. George Donahue's occupation was listed as "salesman." Maureen was a housewife. Both were from the Bronx. He was 34 years old at the time of my birth. She was 29. Her maiden name was listed as Hamilton.

My birth weight was given as eight pounds. I was 20.5 inches long. I had blue eyes, and the color of my hair couldn't be determined at the time.

And on the line for the number of children born alive to my mother prior to my birth, there was a zero, as I had expected.

That was the total of what the records contained. I had to admit it wasn't much to go on. There were no earth-shattering revelations. Nothing that would have caused me to be concerned or unconcerned. On the face of it, I was a very ordinary person. There was nothing extraordinary about me except that I had been placed for adoption. Except for that, no one would think twice about my records.

"I'll make a copy of the page for you," Mrs. Chin told me. "And then we'll take a look at your birth mother's medical records page."

"There's more?" I asked.

"I don't know how much more," Mrs. Chin replied, "but we won't know until we look, will we?"

She loaded a second microfilm reel into the machine and began to turn the handle, stopping at a page for Maureen Donahue.

At first glance, there was nothing suspicious about my birth mother. The page indicated the day she entered the hospital and the day she was discharged. It also listed her father's and mother's names, Theodore and Maureen Hamilton, as well as the name of her attending physician, Dr. Keene.

I thought it was interesting to learn what my grandparents' names were, or had been. But other than that, I didn't see anything out of the ordinary. It wasn't until Mrs. Chin turned to the second page that something took me by surprise. On my birth mother's pregnancy record, just as on my birth record, there was a line for the number of children previously born to her. I expected that line to contain a zero on her record, as it had on mine.

Surprise, surprise! Here was a serious contradiction. Instead of indicating no births prior to mine, the page clearly stated that she had given birth to another child two years before I was born.

That was about the last thing I expected to learn. Down the road, if my search ever did get beyond the confines of St. Clare's, I wouldn't be surprised to learn that my birth mother had had other children after me. But before? That was a scenario I had never anticipated.

Now all I had to decide was which document was correct. I made that decision standing right there next to Mrs. Chin, because it wouldn't take Sherlock Holmes to realize that neglecting to mention an older sibling on my record was the classic red herring. It was an intentional omission, made to keep me from learning the truth. I imagine the doctor in charge never suspected that I would one day compare my records with those of my birth mother.

Suddenly my search seemed to take on a totally new direction. Instead of focusing on my birth mother, my attention seemed to shift toward this older sibling of mine. Who and where was he or she? Who was the father? George Donahue or some other man? And who was this George Donahue?

Maybe my birth parents had been married at the time my older sibling was born but had been divorced by the time I was born. Or there was the possibility that my birth mother had had her first child out of wedlock and then had married my father and had me.

But if that were the case, why was I placed for adoption? And if my birth parents were married, why did my letter from the Foundling tell me they weren't?

I was very confused. There was absolutely no way I could guess what had happened just from two sets of hospital records. And there was no way I was going to solve the mystery with Mrs. Chin breathing down my back.

She couldn't help but notice I was perplexed.

"Would you like a copy of your birth mother's records?"

There was no doubt in my mind that I wanted a copy of those records. I needed a hard copy so I could take my time and carefully examine every detail.

When Mrs. Chin handed me all the copies, I thanked her profusely before rushing out of the hospital to make my train back to Washington. I remember having this feeling that there was going to be someone standing at the door of the hospital waiting to arrest me for taking unauthorized copies of documents out of the hospital. My heart continued to pound wildly until I was safely seated on the train at Penn Station. But even then, I didn't feel totally out of the woods. I didn't dare take out the hospital records until the train had safely passed through Metro Park, New Jersey. And still, I found myself looking around at my fellow passengers to see if any suspicious faces stared in my direction.

As soon as my heart stopped racing, I settled back and began to go over the documents line-by-line. I didn't have a clue as to how I was going to solve the mystery until I noticed a seemingly insignificant handwritten note on my birth mother's records. Her doctor had written, "Patient is in good condition for just having delivered a nine-pound baby."

The fact that my birth weight had been listed as eight pounds and my birth mother's records had me as a nine-pound baby didn't bother me a bit. What was surprising was that, next to the doctor's note, there was a note indicating how much weight my birth mother had gained during her pregnancy. According to that note, she had gained 15 pounds.

So what? Big deal? Why would such a bit of trivia cause me to think I had stumbled across some solid clue? Call it experience. Not personal, but first-hand experience anyway. Because my wife, Patty, and I had three children by this time, I knew a little something about a mother's weight gain during pregnancy, especially the weight gained when a big baby was to be delivered. Of our three children, the smallest baby weighed more than eight pounds at birth, and the biggest tipped the hospital scales at slightly more than ten pounds.

In any case, a woman who delivers a baby of more than eight pounds would, under ordinary circumstances, gain more than 15 pounds. I'd even go so far as to say that a 20- to 25-pound weight gain would be more likely, with a larger gain not too unusual. To gain only 15 pounds and deliver a nine-pound baby was something else again. There had to be more here than met the casual eye.

By the time the train had pulled out of Trenton, I had solved the mystery to my satisfaction. Mrs. Maureen Donahue was not married. Or at least, she wasn't married at the time she was carrying me. Her low weight gain clearly indicated that she actually had done everything in her power to lose weight. Her own weight. By losing some of her own normal weight, she had been able to conceal the fact that she was pregnant. And whatever weight I represented merely looked insigificant on her and could, with proper loose-fitting clothing, be hidden.

Elementary, my dear Watson? Yes; however, where did my amateur sleuthing get me? I was still Washington-bound on a speeding Metroliner with a minor accumulation of raw data. All that I knew and all that I had learned in the past twenty-four hours added up to a paltry sum of relevant information.

Other than the existence of an older sibling, I had discovered nothing more about the circumstances surrounding my birth. In fact, I knew even less than I had known before. For what I had always assumed to be the case—that I had been born out of wedlock to two young lovers—was on the evidence no longer true. Even after I added up all the known and unknown quantities on a sheet of paper, I couldn't arrive at any solid conclusions.

As my train pulled out of Baltimore, I realized that I had come to a major crossroads in my nascent search. The question was, could I live with what I had learned by going to St. Clare's, or would I not be satisfied until I discovered all the missing links?

I quickly decided that I had to take the next step. I had to learn the who, the what, and the why, no matter what. And if I couldn't learn everything, I would definitely settle for learning whatever there was to learn.

My only problem was how to do it.

CHAPTER THREE

Easier Said Than Done

"HOW," I ASKED my wife, "am I going to make sense out of all this and do something about it?"

Photocopies of all the documents I had picked up at St. Clare's were spread out on the kitchen table. I had just finished telling her the story of how I had obtained both my birth records and my birth mother's medical records.

She was as dumbfounded as I was to learn that there had been another baby before me. Patty, too, had assumed that if I had had any brothers or sisters, they would have come after me, not before.

She looked at me across the table. "It's not at all what you expected, is it?"

"To tell you the truth," I said, "I don't really know what I expected."

That wasn't totally true. I had, whether I wanted to admit it or not, wanted the fairy-tale version of my origins—that my birth parents worked in the theater—to come true. It was adventure and romance I was looking for. It was the extraordinary, not the ordinary, that I had hoped to stumble upon at St. Clare's. Deep down, I was a bit disappointed with what I had uncovered, but only because it didn't fit into the mental picture I had long ago painted of my birth parents. There was this wish fulfillment thing I had hoped for. I'd hoped to learn not just the identity of my birth parents, but also that they were each somebody I knew, somebody famous. I had gone in search of gods only to discover mere mortals. And that meant I, too, was only mortal.

"Look on the positive side," Patty told me. "You learned more about your background in one day than many adoptees learn in a lifetime."

She was right. How many stories had I read of adoptees searching all their lives for even the smallest clue to their origins, only to become resigned and go to their graves never knowing anything about their beginnings?

I wanted more.

"Do you think I should look for my birth parents?"

Patty looked at me. She didn't have to say anything.

I looked straight back at her and said, "I know what you're thinking. You're thinking that there's no way in hell I'm not going to look for them."

She smiled and nodded.

"There's no telling what I might find," I explained. "It could be ugly. My birth mother could be a bag lady or even a prostitute."

"That's the risk you're going to have to take."

"And what if she is a bag lady," I pointed out to Patty, "and she wants to come home and live with us?"

Again Patty didn't answer, because she knew I was being ridiculous. In the first place, it would be virtually impossible for me to find my birth mother if she had become a bag lady. And even if I did learn she was living on the streets, there was little chance that I would be able to develop any real relationship with her. A person who has lived on the street as long as my birth mother might have had to, would probably have serious mental problems.

As to my birth mother being a prostitute, it was possible but not very likely. She was probably a very ordinary woman. And that's what made the next step in finding the missing links all that much harder. There was a very good chance my birth mother had married. And if she had, what would it do to her life if I turned up on her doorstep? It could ruin her life, especially if she had never told her family about me. I didn't want to disrupt her life in that way. I didn't have the right to extend my rights to the point of destroying her life. That, more than anything else, was what held me back from plunging into my search with unbridled zeal.

I was looking for assurances, guarantees that my search would not interfere with anyone else's life. The reality of what I was doing carried no assurances, and I knew that. I had to learn to accept certain basic facts before I embarked on the real adoption search. I had to realize that my search could be futile. I had to accept the fact that the names on the birth records might have been fictional. I had to be willing to devote time to following leads until those leads stopped at dead ends, or to follow any new branch-off leads that I might uncover.

How much time I could spend on my search was something else I had to think about. Was I willing to spend months, or possibly even years, in my pursuit? I quickly realized I wasn't willing to devote my life's energy to my search. I had a wife and three children, a job, and some career aspirations. They were all more important than my search, especially if it meant that search was going to be too time-consuming.

I decided that I would take each step as it came,

and after that step, I would evaluate what I had learned and where the next step was most likely to lead me. And all the time, I would have to keep in mind the privacy of the people for whom I was searching.

Not wanting to overstep my bounds, I vowed that the closer I got to locating either of my birth parents, the more diligent I would become in making sure I would not be an unwelcome guest in their lives.

If I detected any negative vibrations, I would back off immediately. I would end my search before bringing any shame, hurt, or humiliation to the lives of innocent people.

With those resolutions firmly made, I was prepared to embark on my search. I was prepared for almost anything, with one exception—death. I had never wanted to admit consciously that my search might lead to my learning that either one or both of my birth parents had died. Death was a possibility, but I decided not to dwell on that likelihood. Rather, I decided to play that hand when and if I were dealt it.

And so I was off. Not with a mighty "Heigho, Silver, and away we go," but with a "Here goes nothing." Lackluster? Guilty as charged, but I didn't want to get my hopes up too high.

Where did I start my search? In Midtown Manhattan. About three weeks after my encounter with Mrs. Chin at St. Clare's, I was in New York on another business trip. Before I checked out of the hotel, I went to a hidden corner of the lobby where the phones were located. I flipped open a copy of the Bronx phone book and quickly turned to the page where the Donahues were listed. As soon as I was sure nobody was looking, I surreptitiously removed that page and stuffed it into my coat pocket.

A hurried glance over my left shoulder assured me nobody from hotel security had seen my dastardly deed. And so the coast was clear for me to perform the same surgery on the page listing the Hamiltons, just in case my birth mother still used her maiden name.

With two pages from the Bronx directory safely hidden in my coat pocket, I made a quick exit and headed toward Penn Station. Having more than a half-hour to kill before I could board my train, I took the jagged-edged papers from my pocket. My eyes immediately caught a listing for a Maureen Donahue.

"Could it be happening this easily?" I thought as I reached instinctively into my pocket for a dime to make a phone call. As fast as I approached one of the empty telephone booths, I stopped in my tracks.

"What am I doing?" I said aloud. "What if this Maureen Donahue answers the phone? What do I tell her? Who do I tell her is calling?"

I backed away from the bank of telephones, the dime still in my hand.

"Think," I kept saying over and over to myself. "Wasn't the moral of one of Aesop's fables, 'Look before you leap?' Yes, it was," I agreed, "and curiosity also killed the cat, but satisfaction brought him back."

Ten minutes passed. The dime was growing hot and sweaty in the palm of my hand. With a gulp that everyone within ten feet of me must have heard, I plunked the glistening dime into the coin slot of the phone and dialed the number of Maureen Donahue.

If she happened to answer I was going to say I was looking for a Maureen Donahue who was the former Maureen Hamilton. If she told me she was the former

Miss Hamilton, I would lie and tell her I was doing some research on the Hamilton family tree. I hoped she would then know instinctively who I was and do the dirty work for me.

She would say, "Son, is that you?"

And I would say, "Yes."

That's what I planned to do. But that's not what happened.

Maureen Donahue's phone rang the requisite three times before a voice came on the line.

"The number you have dialed, 555-6749, is no longer in service. Please check the directory or call an operator for assistance."

I listened to the nasal-toned recording twice before hanging up.

"No longer in service? How is that possible?"

My first thought was that she had moved. My next thought was that my first thought was wrong. People who move usually make arrangements with the phone company to have a recording giving the caller the new number. That's what I did whenever I moved. So I presumed everyone else did it, too.

When I finally did hang up the receiver, I had to admit to my first defeat. Too much of what had already transpired had been the result of a lot of luck. To expect my lucky streak to keep going on an endless roll was unrealistic.

In that sense, then, I was lucky my phone call to Maureen Donahue hadn't connected, because if it had, I would have been buffered by this false sense of invincibility. And that would not have prepared me for any of the pitfalls that might be lurking on the untraveled road ahead of me. Better, I remember thinking, that it be a little more difficult to get in touch with Maureen Donahue.

Better, but I was back to the "how" question again. How was I going to find the telephone number of a woman who didn't leave a trace? She might have changed her phone number to avoid crank calls, or maybe she had moved to another part of the city.

With only a few minutes left before I had to make a run for my train, I called Information for Manhattan, Queens, Brooklyn, Staten Island, and even Long Island, and Westchester and Rockland Counties. There wasn't a single Maureen Donahue listed. There were, however, a lot of M. Donahues. Too many of them to start calling all of them to locate a Maureen.

As I sat on the train, looking out at the marshy meadowlands of New Jersey, a depressing thought hit me. "What if," I proposed to myself, "Maureen Donahue didn't leave a new phone number because where she's gone she doesn't need a phone? What if Maureen Donahue has died?"

That would really mean I was up against a dead end—pun intended. That would certainly mean I'd have no way ever of finding out if Maureen Donahue was the woman for whom I was looking. Unless . . .

Unless she had died only recently. And that had to be it. I'd convinced myself of that by the time my train had passed through New Brunswick. Why? Because her name was listed in the current telephone directory. People who have been long dead usually don't have their names listed in new directories.

So, with that brilliant new thought in mind, I had a new course of action to take. I decided I would call the New York City Department of Vital Statistics and ask if they could tell me if a certain Maureen Donahue of the Bronx had recently passed away.

What could have been easier? As it turned out, it would have been far easier to milk a chicken than try to get an intelligent answer from the half-witted clerk I had to deal with at the Vital Statistics office.

"Good afternoon, Vital Statistics. Miss Diverna speaking. May I help you?"

The woman sounded pleasant and helpful enough.

"Yes," I said. "I was wondering—if I were to give you the name and address of an individual from the Bronx, would you be able to tell me if that person had died?"

A simple and straightforward request, but not for Miss Diverna.

"If," Miss Diverna explained very matter-of-factly, "you can give me the deceased's date of death, I'll verify it for you."

For a quick minute I thought I had reached a government employee with a sense of humor. All I had to do was tell this woman when Maureen Donahue had died, and she'd tell me whether or not Maureen Donahue was dead.

"Maybe I didn't ask the right question," I said to Miss Diverna. "You see, I need for you to tell me if this certain person has died."

"The only way," Miss Diverna responded, "I can tell you if a person has died is if you can tell me when that person died."

I knew it. I hadn't called the Department of Vital Statistics. I had dialed a number in the Twilight Zone, and I was actually talking to Rod Serling's secretary.

Trying not to laugh, I asked Miss Diverna, "Are

you telling me the only way you can tell me if someone has died is if I can tell you when they died?"

"That's correct," she said.

I tried to reason with her. "Why would I be calling you to verify a person's death if I knew when that person had died?"

"I don't know why you'd be calling me," she stated, "but we have our procedures to follow."

So much for governmental red tape. I had heard it was difficult cutting through it, but I didn't know it was so sticky. Now I was back to square one. I didn't have a new phone number for Maureen Donahue, if in fact she had one, and I didn't know whether she was dead or alive. I mulled over my position for a day or two, almost ready to give up on Maureen, when another thought struck me.

Maybe Maureen was still alive. Maybe she had moved to another state. And if she had, more than likely she would have arranged with the Post Office to have her mail forwarded to her new address.

If only I could find that new address. But how?

The answer to my question came on a Monday morning when I asked Dennis Burkhardt, a colleague in Washington, if he could help. Dennis had worked for the U.S. Post Office Department, and I thought there might be a way for him to find out if Maureen Donahue had left a new address. I gave him the information I had on Maureen's last listed address and started crossing my fingers, because considering the luck I had just had with one governmental office, I wasn't expecting too much from the Post Office. In fact, I imagined some clerk telling Dennis that if he could provide Maureen Donahue's new address, they'd verify it for him. That wasn't the case at all, however: Dennis appeared at my desk before lunch that day and handed me a slip of paper.

"Maureen Donahue now lives in Phoenix. Her address is in care of Richard Donahue. He must be her son."

I thanked Dennis for his detective work and immediateliy called Phoenix Directory Assistance, asking for Maureen's number. The next thing I knew, I was dialing her number, and before I could talk myself out of making the call, a woman answered the phone.

"Hello," the voice said.

She had a nice voice. I pictured this wonderful woman with slightly graying hair and a warm smile. The woman I was really picturing was my own mother, Catherine Begley, and that was a strange feeling that hadn't occurred to me until I placed that call to Maureen Donahue. I realized that the only image I had of a "mother" was the image of my own mother. No matter how hard I tried to picture my birth mother another way, I would always see a mental picture of my mother.

That's who I thought I was talking to when I said to the woman who picked up the phone, "I hope I'm not disturbing you, but I'm trying to locate Maureen Donahue."

"I'm Maureen Donahue."

"Are you the former Maureen Hamilton from the Bronx?"

"No," was all she said, and all she needed to say.

After thanking her, I hung up the receiver, crumpled the piece of paper with her name and address on it, and tossed it in a trash can.

Maureen Donahue was alive and well and living in

Phoenix, and I had come up against a real dead end.

I had wasted some time in my pursuit of Maureen Donahue, but I hadn't wasted nearly as much time as many of the adoptees who spend years following up clues that lead nowhere.

There was, if anything, a lesson in my dead-end search for Maureen Donahue. I learned that my adoption search was not something that was going to be easy. Nothing was going to be handed to me on a silver platter. If I were to be successful, it was going to take a combination of luck, diligence, patience, and perseverance. It also meant using the clues I had to their best advantage.

I took the telephone pages listing the Donahues and Hamiltons out of my desk drawer and tossed them in the trash can alongside Maureen Donahue's phone number. No sooner had I done that than I bent down and picked the listing for the Hamiltons out of the trash. I smoothed out the wrinkles on the stolen sheets of paper and stared at the first Hamilton phone number on the page.

The next thing I knew, I was dialing that number.

My search was on again.

CHAPTER FOUR

*Doing It By the Book
or For Whom the Telephone Bell Tolls*

DID I HAVE a prepared speech when I picked up the phone to make a call to the first Hamilton in the Bronx? No. I was as prepared, or unprepared, as I was when I called the unsuspecting Maureen Donahue in Phoenix. I did, however, have an approach this time, as unsophisticated as that approach might be. I had decided that when and if someone answered the phone I would say I was looking for a Maureen Donahue, the former Maureen Hamilton.

I used that simple indirect query, knowing full well that Maureen Hamilton probably never had become Maureen Donahue. But that didn't matter. What mattered was that I was comfortable with my little ploy. Comfortable enough not to hang up when I heard the ring at the other end on the first number I dialed.

The ringing stopped. A man answered, "Hello."

"I was wondering," I said in perfect honesty, "if you could help me. I'm looking for a Maureen Donahue, the former Maureen Hamilton."

He didn't even pause. "Sorry, don't know anybody by that name."

He hung up before I had a chance to ask him anything else.

My second call didn't go much better. The third

number I dialed was busy, and the fourth Hamilton in the book wasn't home when I phoned.

The fifth call raised my hopes a bit. Again, a man answered, but there was something about his voice. I could tell by the way he sounded that he wouldn't cut me off with a brusque, "Sorry."

When I asked him if he knew of a Maureen Hamilton who had become a Donahue, he thought a moment.

"We're a pretty big family," he told me. "Let me think if there was a Maureen."

He thought for another moment while I patiently waited for him to scan his family tree.

"I can't recall offhand if there ever was a Maureen Hamilton. Maybe my wife might know."

My cooperative answerer must have put his hand over the mouthpiece, because his voice was muffled as he called to his wife and asked if she could remember ever having heard of a Maureen Hamilton in their family. His wife was too far away from the phone for me to hear her reply.

"I thought we had something there," he told me when he came back on the line, "but my wife was confusing my second cousin Doreen with Maureen. Sorry I can't be more helpful."

"You've been more than helpful," I told him, as he wished me good luck in finding Maureen Hamilton Donahue.

I went back to the third number I had dialed to see if the phone was still busy. It was. And the party at the fourth number hadn't returned home.

After making some notations in the column next to the names, I dialed the sixth number on the list. I was about to hang up when a groggy voice came on the line.

At first I thought I was calling too early, but it was after ten o'clock in the morning.

"I hope I'm not disturbing you," I began, "but I was wondering if you might be able to help me. I'm doing some family research, and I'm trying to locate a Maureen Donahue who is the former Maureen Hamilton. Do you have a relative by that name?"

"You must want my grandmother. She lives in the Bronx, but she's away right now."

There was something wrong. Judging from the sound of this person's voice, he must have been in his twenties. And if that were true, there would be no way my birth mother could be his grandmother.

"Was your grandmother's maiden name Hamilton?" I asked, again wondering what his reply would be.

"No, Hamilton is her married name."

"I see. Well, the Maureen I'm looking for is a much younger woman."

"Maybe you want my Aunt Mo."

That was interesting. Not because his grandmother and aunt had the same name, but because, according to my birth mother's hospital documents, both she and her mother were named Maureen. Of course, it could have been a coincidence, so I looked on the hospital form where it listed my grandmother's maiden name. It was Gilhooley.

"I don't know if we're talking about the same Maureen Hamilton, but could you tell me what your grandmother's maiden name was?"

He paused for a moment before he answered.

"Gilhooley," was all he had to say to let me know I had struck gold.

"I must have the right number, because the Maureen Donahue I'm looking for had a mother whose maiden name was also Gilhooley.''

"You must be talking about my Aunt Mo, then, but her name isn't Donahue. It's still Hamilton. Aunt Mo isn't married.''

That confirmed many of my suspicions.

"Could you tell me why you're looking for my aunt?'' he asked.

"You see,'' I told him, measuring each of my words carefully, "I believe I'm your Aunt Mo's son.''

There was a very dramatic pause on his end of the line. Every trace of grogginess left his voice as he came back to life.

"I think you'd better talk to my father,'' he said.

I immediately thought I had said the wrong thing. And, in hindsight, I probably should have gone about explaining my identity a little more carefully. But it was too late. I had said what I had to say.

I half expected to hear a raging voice come on the line, but to my surprise the voice was very calm and understanding.

"My son just told me who you are,'' the older voice said.

"I didn't mean to upset you,'' I replied.

"You didn't upset me. But I think you'd be better off if you talked to my sister Joan. She's much better at handling things like this. I'll give you her phone number.''

My new-found uncle gave me Aunt Joan's home telephone number, which in itself was an act of faith. How did he know I wasn't some crackpot? How could he be sure I wasn't going to start making crank phone calls to his sister? For whatever reason, he was willing to allow me to take my search to the next and very important step.

I was very close to cracking the case wide open if Aunt Joan was as cooperative as my uncle was. Again I was dealing with the "if" word. A word that was so small, but could stand between me and my ultimate goal.

There was no telling how Joan was going to react to my unexpected bombshell. I couldn't imagine that my uncle wasn't going to give her a call to warn her about me. Such a warning could easily have spelled disaster. I wouldn't have been surprised if Joan had become angry at my impertinence. Or she might have reacted by becoming very protective of her sister Maureen. Dozens of scenarios raced through my head all that afternoon as I braced myself for the inevitable phone call that evening.

Patty was surprised that I had managed to get so close to finding my birth mother in such a short period of time. She made sure the kids were down in the family room when I went to make the call to Joan from the phone in our bedroom. I needed all the peace and quiet possible. What I didn't need was to have one of my kids walk into the room while I was on the phone with Joan. My wife closed the door to our family room just as I closed our bedroom door.

It was the calm before the storm. I sat on the edge of our bed staring down at the phone on the night table. My hand temporarily refused to leave my side. It seemed to have a mind of its own.

I could feel my heart beating. My hands began to tremble as a sudden nervous chill ran up and down my back, causing me to shiver.

With a gulp and a deep breath, I ordered my hand

to pick up the phone. I dialed the number. It was busy.

I must have listened to the busy signal for a good minute, because it was a comforting sound. It was my reprieve, and I began to understand how a person on death row must feel when the governor calls.

My reprieve was very short-lived. When I dialed the number again a few minutes later, the phone was no longer busy. The woman I came to know as Aunt Joan answered the phone. Her voice was very distinct. Very clear and very much in control. My voice was jumpy and a pitch higher than normal.

After telling her who I was, I said, "I hope I'm not calling you at a bad time."

She assured me I wasn't. She had been expecting my phone call. And in fact, she had just been talking with one of her sisters before I called.

"I hope my call to your brother didn't upset him. Or upset you, for that matter."

"I'd be lying if I didn't say I was surprised. But not shocked," Joan said calmly, measuring each word as she spoke.

"It wouldn't have surprised me if you had told me to go away and mind my own business. I mean, there's no way you can be sure I'm not making all this up."

"I don't think you'd make up something like this," she said.

"I'm glad you feel that way."

"Please tell me," she said slowly, "your date of birth."

"I was born July 11, 1948."

I waited for what seemed an eternity after telling her that.

"Is there something wrong?" I finally asked,

breaking the long silence.

"No," she answered with some hesitation, "I was just trying to remember something."

"Did you ever know about me?"

"Before your call, you mean?"

"Yes. Did you or anybody else in your family know that your sister had had a child and placed it for adoption?"

"I can't say for sure. I know I didn't know about you."

It was hard for me not to ask questions about the other child. As far as I knew he or she might have been raised by my birth mother.

"Your mother doesn't live in New York anymore. She moved to South Carolina eight years ago."

"She never married, did she?"

"Maureen and I are both single. The rest got married."

"How many were there in your family?"

"There were thirteen of us. Six boys and seven girls. There are only ten of us now. Nana, your grandmother, is alive. She's up with one of my sisters. She's recovering from an operation on her hip."

Joan continued to fill me in on some of the family history. By the time she started naming the grandchildren in the family, I was a bit boggled. When Joan finished with the first installment of the Hamilton-Gilhooley family history, I gave her a brief rundown on my family.

She was very interested to learn about my children, and I could tell she was very fond of children. I could hear it in her voice. I never brought up the subject of my birth father. Joan took care of that.

"What have you learned about your father?" she

asked.

"Nothing really. According to the records I have, his name is George Donahue."

It was at that instant that I wished she and I had television attachments on our telephones, because I needed to be able to judge her facial reaction when she heard my birth father's name. She was probably a good poker player, because her voice didn't give away anything. Joan only repeated his name to me.

"Did you know him?"

"I think I knew your birth father."

That was all she said before she carefully directed our conversation away from my birth father. I took the subtle hint and didn't pursue that line of questioning. There'd be time for that later. If there was a later.

I wasn't sure if my search had reached its conclusion or not with my phone call to Joan. She assured me she wanted to talk more about it, but she asked if I could give her a week to sort it all out.

"Call me next Sunday night about this same time," she told me. "We'll talk more then."

When I hung up, I sat on the edge of the bed for a few minutes before going downstairs to tell Patty about my conversation with Aunt Joan.

I had learned a lot. I had learned only a little. There were still many more links for me to find before I could be satisfied that I had learned about as much as there was to learn.

My search for those missing links in my life was no longer a hypothetical one. It was real. The cast of characters was now expanding.

Would I ever meet my birth mother? Was I to learn who George Donahue was? Would there be a happy ending?

I wondered. And I waited the longest week in my life before I found myself on the phone with Aunt Joan again.

PART TWO
And You Shall Find

If Ponce de Leon found the
fountain of youth,
why did he grow old
and die?

A young student's
rhetorical historical
question.

CHAPTER FIVE

A Month of Sundays

WAITING THAT FULL week until I made my second call to Joan was pure torture. I couldn't seem to keep my mind on anything but that pending phone call. And while I was waiting for the other shoe to drop, I developed a rash from head to toe. Even my itches had itches.

An allergy? No, I wasn't allergic to anything. It was a common case of the jitters. Whether I wanted to admit it or not, I was a nervous wreck all that week. Anticipation was the culprit, but guilt also played its part. And it was the guilt I had the hardest time dealing with, the guilt that came from still not having broken the news about my search to my parents. What made the guilt weigh even heavier was the fact that most of my friends, neighbors, and co-workers knew about my search. I'd never had any intention of hiding my search from my parents. I had planned on telling them when the moment was right.

According to the original script I had drafted, I would have spent a much longer time on the initial search than it had actually taken. On my hypothetical search schedule, I had figured in the appropriate time to mention my activity casually to my mother and father. I say casually, because I had never expected to get as far as I had. I had thought all I'd be telling my parents was about my trip to St. Clare's and all the wrong telephone calls I had made. Little did I know I'd have to tell them I'd located my birth mother's family. But to have called them after my first phone call with Joan would have been premature. It was the content of the second phone call that would be all-telling and all-knowing. At least that's how I reasoned it out to myself and to my sister Patti.

"I don't think you have anything to worry about," Patti said when I phoned her and told her about my talk with Joan.

"If only I could be certain," I replied.

"When I talked to Mom the other night, I told her all about the information I got from the Foundling. And do you know what she said? She told me she wouldn't be surprised if you went looking for your birth mother someday."

My mother had an uncanny ability to anticipate the future. She had no clairvoyant abilities, but she did have a very accurate seventh sense. It didn't surprise me that she thought I would one day undertake an adoption search. What did surprise me was that she had talked about it with my sister when I was at the zenith of my search.

"You have to remember," my sister pointed out, "that Mom reads *Good Housekeeping* and *Redbook*. They both have had lots of articles on adoption, so I'm sure she must have thought about it as far as we were concerned. And as she told me, 'Vincent has always been very curious about everything. I can't see how he wouldn't be curious about his mother.'"

"Could you get a feel for how she'd react if I did search?"

"I asked her. I asked her how she'd feel if either you or I were to locate our birth parents."

"And what did she say?"

"She told me it wouldn't bother her in the least."

That was my mother. She never felt threatened by human emotion. As far as she was concerned, she had done her job as a mother. And a good job she had done, too. Why would she have to feel threatened? My birth mother couldn't take away all the years of mothering my mother had showered on both my sister and me.

My mother wasn't in competition with anybody. She had earned her rightful place as my mother. And I think she knew that I would not be searching to replace her.

In fact, if there was a definite contributing source for my search, I could point back to my mother with pride. She had given me a great sense of what it meant to be a mother. She had taught me the essence of motherhood, what it meant and what it didn't mean. And because she had filled me with this sense, I had gone through life with her definition in mind, and I had also applied it to the woman who had brought me into this world.

That woman, too, was my "mother." But not in the same sense that my mother—my adoptive mother—was. There was a difference. One woman gave me life; the other gave me living. I couldn't have survived with one and not the other. The fact that it had taken two women to accomplish what is normally the role of only one did not lessen either of their singular gifts. On the contrary, they had shared accomplishments. They had a link that bound them together as much as the links that bound each of them to me.

What remained to be found was why there were two mothers in my life.

Knowing how my mother felt about my adoption search lessened the degree of my guilt, but it didn't make my rash go away. Anticipation was still the culprit. And the anticipation only aggravated my rash, because I grew more and more anxious as the calendar crept slowly toward that Sunday night when I was to make that all-important phone call.

After letting my Aunt Joan's phone ring a dozen times at the mutually agreed-upon hour, I hung up and began calling back at ten-minute intervals. I arbitrarily picked 11:00 p.m. as the last time I would try to reach her. Fortunately, I didn't have to wait that long or make that many phone calls before Joan answered her phone.

She was full of apologies. She had been over to her brother's house and had gotten a late start back home.

"So, how are you?" she asked, sounding more like an old friend than a stranger.

"Fine," I said, deciding not to go into detail about my rash.

"That's good to hear," she said.

She paused for a moment, I think to get a cigarette.

"I gave our phone call last week a lot of thinking. I told you then I wasn't shocked about the news, but I was startled. You see, I did have this feeling that Maureen had had a baby. I wanted to think I was wrong, but deep down I knew I was right. I guess I just didn't want to admit it. But . . ."

I waited some thirty seconds before she continued talking.

"There's something else I need to know," she started fresh. "Was there anything else you learned from your hospital records?''

I knew instinctively what she was getting at. Yet I was afraid to be the one actually to put into words the subject of the other child.

"Well," I started to say. Joan interrupted me.

"There was another child before you. That's the child I thought I knew about. But when you told me when you had been born, I was very confused. I had expected you to tell me you had been born in 1945, not 1948."

"I can understand why you were surprised. I was surprised, too."

"It explains a lot about your mother."

I didn't know if I was the "it" or if both my sibling and I were the "it" my aunt was talking about. That's because we only skirted the issue of my birth mother. Both Joan and I were treating her like a fragile Dresden china doll.

When it came to imagining this woman who was my birth mother, I couldn't help but see her living the life of a cloistered nun.

I mustered up enough courage to ask directly about her. "Is there something you can't tell me about my mother?"

I actually expected Joan to give me the name and address of the convent where my birth mother was living.

"Your mother is a very private person. She always managed to keep her distance from the rest of the family. When holidays like Christmas and Thanksgiving came around, she never really wanted to get together with the family. She even used to say that she was depressed at Christmas."

"That's not uncommon," I remarked. "There are

a lot of people who hate Christmas because everyone around them is enjoying it so much and they can't.''

"Knowing now what Mo's been through, I can understand why she built a wall around herself and didn't want to let anybody in.''

"Considering you might eventually tell her about me, how do you think she'll react?''

"You just might prove to be what she's needed all these years. You might be able to bring down that wall of hers.''

I didn't know it then, but there was a role reversal in my adoption search. From what I had read about adoptees in search, those adoptees found what they needed when they located a birth parent. Little did I realize that it was possible for the adoptee to be the key to a birth parent's new lease on life.

I was reminded of a passage from Saint-Exupery's *The Little Prince* when the Little Prince talks about taming the fox and how you become responsible for the things you tame. If I were to play a part, no matter how small that part might prove to be, in leading my birth mother into the family, I was going to have to bear some of the responsibility for her future. Of course all that was *in* the future, but I had the glimmer of an instinct when Joan was telling me about my birth mother.

Both Aunt Joan and I realized that talking on the phone was not the way to accomplish anything significant. There was a definite need to talk face-to-face.

What little ground we had covered on the phone was enough to establish our true identities. I could sense certain commendable qualities in Joan. And I guess she could sense that I was not some drifter whose only intent was to disrupt her sister's life. She had nothing to fear from meeting me and I had all to gain by meeting her.

We ended our conversation by discussing my position in the family's birth order. Joan told me that Virginia and her husband were living with my birth mother at the time she was pregnant with me.

"Your Aunt Virginia was pregnant at the time, too. And I guess because everyone was thinking about her baby, they didn't pay too much attention to your mother. In fact, now that I think back on it, I do remember your mother had put on some weight around that time, but none of us took special note of it."

"When," I asked Joan, "did Virginia have her baby?"

"Your cousin Ted was born on July 23rd, less than two weeks after you were born."

"Is my mother close to him today?"

"She's very close to him, and he's particularly fond of your mother. They almost have a mother and son relationship."

"I can understand that," I said. "Ted was a logical replacement for me. In one way, that was a blessing, because she could shower her affection on a child, even if it wasn't her own child. But in another way, it was sad because Ted would always remind her of the child she had given up."

Talking about Ted reminded me of the time span in my early months when the Foundling had no record of me. I wondered if Joan knew anything about those first few months.

"Do you remember what my mother did after I was born?"

"That was a long time ago," she answered.

"I understand, but is there anything you might re-member?"

She paused. "Let me see. Oh, one thing: she and Virginia didn't live together after you were born. Your mother had her own place."

"Did my mother live with her sister up until the time she delivered me?"

"No. Your mother went away for a time. I think she went to Atlantic City or someplace like that."

"She just went away, no questions asked?"

"I know it sounds peculiar, but you have to re-member there were so many of us. If one of us wasn't getting married, someone was having a baby. The War was just over. My brothers were getting out of the serv-ice. One or the other of us was moving from one place to another. So we didn't take special note if somebody dropped out for a little while."

It all did sound a bit bizarre to me, but I didn't know the situation well enough to make an appropriate comment on how it would be possible for someone to just drop out for a little while, have a baby, and then drop back in.

"When Mo did come back, she started to do some volunteer work for Doctor Keene."

Doctor Keene was the physician who had deliv-ered me.

"She also started spending time doing volunteer work at the Foundling Home."

Talk about returning to the scene of the crime. It seemed that my birth mother was trying to cope with the situation by staying close to it, instead of distancing herself from it. I would have thought she'd have wanted to forget everything about the experience.

"Did anybody think that odd?"

"Not really," Joan said. "Doctor Keene was considered part of our family. He delivered you, Mo's other baby, Ted, and a few of my other sisters' children."

"Obviously he knew all about what was going on."

"I'm sure he did, but he was an honorable man. He wouldn't have said anything to anybody."

My head began to spin with all the bits and pieces that were coming at me from all angles.

I told Joan I was going to be in New York the following Thursday. I wondered if she would be able to get together with me.

"I could take the train down after work and meet you in Grand Central," Joan said. "We could have dinner together."

"We could meet right under the big clock opposite the information booth on the main level," I told her, remembering all those old movies with people meeting under the big clock.

"I can get there around 6:30."

"I'll be there."

It dawned on me then that I had no idea what Joan looked like.

"How will I recognize you?" I asked.

"I'm rather tall, and I have light brown hair. I wear glasses. And I'll probably be wearing my camel-colored coat."

With the exception of the coat, she could have been describing me.

"I'll find you," I said.

"It will be good to meet you," Joan said. "I'm looking forward to it."

"Me, too," I said before ending our long phone

conversation.

Funny. After hanging up the receiver, my rash no longer itched. The phone call did what none of the ointments could do, and that was ease my mind.

After sorting out some of the information, and writing down a few notes, I went downstairs and told Patty about the latest step in my adoption adventure. When I finished talking, she had a puzzled look on her face.

"What," she asked, "about your father? Did she tell you anything about him?"

Patty couldn't believe I hadn't asked about him, but when I explained that I didn't want to appear too pushy for information, she seemed to understand—half-heartedly.

"You'll ask about him when you meet with your aunt, won't you?"

"If the moment is right," I said. "I'll ask about him. But you have to remember, Joan might not even know who George Donahue was, if in fact that's who my birth father was."

"There's so much more you need to know," Patty remarked.

And she was right. I had learned a lot. I had learned a little. But all of what I had learned were only pieces of a bigger puzzle. My first encounter with Joan was going to be a crucial step in putting some of those pieces together. I tried to fit some of them together mentally as I drifted off to sleep that night.

Unfortunately, none of them seemed to fit, because I was forcing them together. I didn't have a clear enough picture to make any sense out of the individual pieces. I had to be patient.

"Six-thirty under the big clock in Grand Central," I said to myself as I gave in to the sandman. "Six-thirty. Big Clock. Grand Central . . . Grand Central . . . Grand . . ."

Finally to sleep. Perchance to dream.

CHAPTER SIX

Come Out . . . Come Out . . . Wherever You Are

NEVER PLAN ON meeting someone you've never seen before near the big clock in Grand Central Terminal at 6:30 in the evening. The only way I can describe Grand Central at that hour is to ask you to imagine rats fleeing a sinking cargo vessel on the high seas.

To avoid being trampled to death, as well as to avoid being swept along with the crowd and shoved on a train bound for Stamford, I huddled against the side of a telephone booth. But even that safe harbor didn't afford me total protection from the running masses yearning to breathe free. I was poked, jabbed, jostled, and virtually beaten upon as I tried to maintain my ground against the suburban hordes.

A look at my watch told me I had arrived far too early for my own good. It was a little before six when I first positioned myself next to the telephone. When zero hour arrived, I was willing to pass up any medals conferred upon stationary victims who survive the battle of rush-hour, if only I could locate Joan amongst the countless commuters.

The crowd began to dwindle as the hands on the big clock above me moved closer to seven o'clock. Hundreds of women had passed by my safe vantage point. None of them had fit Aunt Joan's self-description. As the hour grew later, however, I began to alter her description to fit more closely my pool of possible suspects.

At first I didn't care what color coat any of the women was wearing. Even though Joan had told me she would be wearing a camel-colored coat, there was a chance that she had changed her mind and decided to wear her blue coat with the fur collar, or her London Fog raincoat, or a ski jacket, or whatever.

I stopped looking at coats and began doing a height inspection. Aunt Joan had claimed she was rather tall. I hadn't questioned her as to her exact height, although I now wished I had, because "rather tall" is a rather inexact measurement. So I discarded the height requirement and began looking for a woman with light brown hair wearing glasses. Do you know how many women there are in Grand Central who have brown hair and wear glasses? I lost count after the twenty-seventh woman with brown hair and glasses walked past me.

It got to the point where I was beginning to imagine that any and every woman who walked within twenty feet of the information booth opposite the big clock was my Aunt Joan. I knew I was beginning to hallucinate when I almost approached a woman I was positive was Aunt Joan. So what if she was only about four feet eleven inches tall with jet black hair, no glasses, and had two Oriental children in tow?

It was a little after seven-thirty when I deposited money in the telephone I called my sanctuary and phoned Joan's apartment. There was no answer. And I was left without a solution to my dilemma.

So I decided to call the cousin I had talked to the

first day I had made contact with the Hamilton clan. He was home. And when I told him my predicament, he laughed. "Aunt Joan is always late," he said, "but if she told you she'd meet you, she'll be there sometime."

I then decided to call my wife in Virginia. Maybe she had heard from Joan.

"I thought you'd never call," Patty said when she heard my frantic voice on the phone.

"I told you I was going to call you after I had dinner with my aunt."

"That's just it. She called after you left for New York this morning to tell me she had to cancel out on your dinner tonight because she was going to have to work late on an important last-minute job at her office."

"You knew all along she wasn't going to meet me?"

"That's what I just told you."

"It's almost funny. Here I am standing in the middle of Grand Central Terminal looking at every woman's face to see if she might resemble an aunt I've never seen, and she wasn't going to be here after all. I'm surprised I wasn't arrested."

"Your aunt told me you should give her a call at her place after ten o'clock."

I said good-bye to my wife. It was now seven-thirty. If I ran fast enough, I still had time to get in line at the half-price ticket booth at Duffy Square to get a ticket for a Broadway show. At least that way the evening wouldn't be a total loss.

Because it was a chilly night, there weren't many people in line at the ticket booth. I picked up a ticket for that night's performance of Joseph Papp's *The Pirates of Penzance*. As I watched the first act unfold, I wanted to warn the young pirate prince that if he ever planned on meeting up with his aunt at Grand Central, he should bring along a sandwich, something to drink, and a suit of armor.

During the intermission, I took a gamble that my aunt might have arrived home earlier than she had told my wife she would. My gamble paid off—she was home. She apologized profusely for not meeting me. I told her not to give it a second thought.

"I can't get down to New York tomorrow," she told me. "Is there any chance you might be able to come up here and meet me for lunch?"

The "up here" she was referring to was New Rochelle. The New Rochelle train station was only a few minutes from her office. She had a timetable, so we made arrangements for her to pick me up at the station at 12:19 p.m.

Next morning I had no problem making the train, and the ride was enjoyable. I was half expecting to see my aunt waiting for me on the platform. She wasn't there, though. When the train pulled out, there was nobody on the platform . . . except me.

And I was still there at 12:45.

"It couldn't be happening again," I thought to myself.

It could, but to avoid standing out in the cold any longer than necessary, I called my aunt's office.

"Joan isn't here," the woman on the other end of the line told me. "She left for lunch at noon and said she wouldn't be back until two or two-thirty."

When I told this woman I was the person Joan was supposed to be having lunch with, she didn't sound surprised that I had called.

"Sometimes," this kind woman told me, "Joan is

a little late."

I didn't say anything. I just thanked her and told her if Joan happened to arrive back at work, to give her a message that her nephew had called—the one she was supposed to have lunch with.

Just as I was about to give up on ever meeting with my aunt, a car rounded the corner heading toward the station. Behind the wheel was a woman wearing a camel-colored coat. She had light brown hair, and she wore glasses.

She waved to me as she pulled up beside me.

At once she said, "I'm late, aren't I?"

"Well," I said, not really knowing what else to say.

I got into the car. Aunt Joan looked at me. I could tell she was trying to place me in the Hamilton family tree. I was doing the same thing. I was looking at her to see if I could find a glimmer of a resemblance to me. As soon as I thought I noticed something, it vanished. I guess I was hoping to see a mirror image. I guess I was hoping for too much.

Was I disappointed? Not really. The fact that I was face-to-face with someone from my family was rewarding enough.

I immediately liked my aunt. She had a nice smile. I think she was a bit nervous about the entire ordeal, because she circled the railroad station three times before executing a right-hand turn onto the main road in New Rochelle.

"There's a very good diner near here," she told me as she began to look down the street to see if she could find it. "I don't get out for lunch very much. I usually eat right at my desk. This is a treat."

I didn't say much. Aunt Joan did most of the talking, and she made mostly small talk.

"You must think I'm a real scatter-brain. I'm not always this bad . . . although I do have a reputation."

"So I've learned," I said.

She laughed and shrugged her shoulders.

We hit it off from the beginning. I felt very much at ease with her. Our conversation at lunch was a series of my questions interspersed with hers. We went the full gamut of questions before the waitress brought our lunch.

Aunt Joan was very interested in seeing pictures of my children.

"Do you see a resemblance?" I asked.

She was holding a picture of my son Jeremy.

"It's the red hair," my aunt told me. "My grandmother, your great-grandmother, had red hair. That would be your grandfather's mother. She was born in Germany."

"German?" I thought to myself. "I never thought of myself as German."

I don't know what I had thought of myself as being. I somehow imagined that I was Scandinavian, because I had blue eyes and had had blond hair as a child. But so do many German children.

"Do I look anything like my mother?"

Aunt Joan looked over at me.

"Not really."

Her right hand was folded over her left hand. I looked down and noticed my hands were folded the same way. And it was then that I noticed her hands.

People had always remarked on the length of my fingers. I had the fingers of a pianist.

"We both have the same hands," I told her.

Aunt Joan unfolded her hands and looked at them. She put one hand up against mine.

"You have the Hamilton hands, that's for sure," she said.

In between bites of her sandwich, she asked me questions about my adoption search: where it began, how, and even why.

She seemed satisfied with all my answers, and was generally surprised at how fast my search had gone.

"It's ironic," she told me, "that you have two cousins who were adopted. And they were both adopted from the Foundling Home."

I was surprised to hear that, again, because I had never imagined all the real things about my "other" family.

Aunt Joan told me all about my many other aunts, uncles, and cousins. When the conversation started to turn to the inevitable—my birth father—Joan grew a little uncomfortable.

"You remember how confused I was when we first spoke on the phone? It just wasn't the question about Mo's other baby that bothered me; it was about your father. At first I was convinced I knew who he was. Then I began to have doubts."

Realizing Joan either didn't know much about my birth father or that she didn't feel comfortable talking about him, I sought more information about my sibling.

"Do you know anything about this other child?"

"I wish I could tell you more. I can't even tell you if the child was a boy or a girl, although I have my suspicions it was a boy."

"And the father?" I asked.

"I'm almost positive who the father was."

"Was he my father?"

She shook her head. I had reached a dead end. There was nothing more Aunt Joan and I could do but make plans.

"Where do we go from here?" I asked.

"Your mother was just up here for Thanksgiving. I've been promising her I'd get down to see her. That's when I'm going to tell her about you. I don't think it's something I could tell her over the phone."

"What does your sister Virginia think about all this?"

"She doesn't want to see Maureen get hurt."

"Does she think finding out about me is going to hurt her?"

"Your Aunt Virginia is only being protective. We talked all about it. We're both convinced this might be the best thing for Maureen."

"How do you think your mother is going to react to my turning up?"

"Mom's been through a lot. I'm sure she'll love the idea once she gets used to it."

"Do you think your mother ever suspected?"

"If she did, she never let on."

Joan looked down at her watch.

"We could talk for days, but I better get back to work if I want to keep my job."

When Joan and I said our good-byes at the train station, we parted good friends.

"I'm going to want you to come to dinner at my sister Ruth's house. Do you think you might be able to come up next week?"

"I'm supposed to be up the following week."

"We'll make it the following week then. I'll give

you a call. You can take the train up and I'll pick you up at the station."

When the night of the family dinner arrived I was prepared for Aunt Joan to be late. She surprised me. She was standing on the train platform when I stepped off the train.

Aunt Ruth and Uncle Frank couldn't have been more hospitable. Their youngest daughter, Kathleen, was home for dinner, too. She was the first cousin I met face-to-face.

What could have turned out to be a modern-day edition of the Spanish Inquisition resulted in a nice family meal, a "get to know each other" gathering.

After dinner, Aunt Ruth showed me a family album. There was only one picture of my birth mother in it.

"Your mother never liked her picture taken," Aunt Ruth said.

"She'd be the first one to leave a room when anyone took out a camera," Joan added.

Unfortunately, I couldn't get a clear idea from the picture what my birth mother looked like. I'd have to wait until the time was right. The time when I would see her in person.

Before I left for the train station, the phone rang. It was Virginia. She knew I was going to be at Ruth's for dinner.

"Your Aunt Virginia would like to talk to you," Ruth told me.

"I can't stay on the phone too long," Aunt Virginia said as soon as I had greeted her, "because Mom is beginning to get suspicious with all these secret phone calls going back and forth. I just wanted to say hello."

I think she wished she could have come to dinner at her sister's house that night. She was going to have to settle for a phone call and her sister's review of how I had fared at dinner.

When I finished talking with Virginia, Joan told me the game plan. "I'm going to make reservations to go down and see your mother next week. Virginia's going to come down with me. Once we've told your mother, we'll call you."

That was the plan.

When Uncle Frank took me back to the station, he told me he had a good relationship with my birth mother.

"She's a fine woman," he said, "on the quiet side. Shy maybe, but that's understandable, knowing what she's been through."

I liked Frank. He was down-to-earth and honest. He had a more objective understanding of the situation than my mother's sisters seemed to have. I wondered if he knew anything about my father, so I asked him if he knew my father. He was truthful but vague.

"I knew your father," he said. "He was a real nice guy."

That was all he told me. My train was pulling into the station, so I couldn't ask him more questions. And even if I'd had the time, I don't think Frank would have told me anything more.

All in all, though, I was satisfied with the way things had gone. It would only be a matter of a week before Joan and Virginia were down at my birth mother's.

Not true.

The following week Aunt Joan called to tell me that

Maureen had asked that the trip be postponed.

"Why?" I asked.

"She's having some work done in her apartment. So she'd rather wait until it's finished before we come down."

I was wondering if the meeting would ever take place.

"When do you think you'll get down there?"

"I can't get away from my office again until next month, but I'm definitely making plane reservations tomorrow, whether Virginia can come down with me or not."

And as far as I knew, my aunt did make reservations, and did go down to visit my birth mother. I didn't expect my aunt to tell her about me the minute she arrived, so I wasn't expecting a call from my aunt for at least a day or two.

One night early that week the phone rang. I answered it, not even thinking it might be my aunt. It wasn't.

I first thought it was a wrong number, because there was a silence on the other end after I said "Hello." As I was about to hang up, I heard someone speaking very softly, almost inaudibly.

The voice simply said, "Hello. This is your mother."

CHAPTER SEVEN

The Best Laid Plans

IT WASN'T SUPPOSED to happen that way at all. Joan was supposed to call me from my birth mother's. She was going to get on the phone and say, "Vincent, I'm at your mother's house. I'd like you to say hello to her."

Joan might have used different words, but the effect would have been the same. I would have been prepared. As it turned out, I was totally unprepared. I was in a state of shock.

I could tell from my birth mother's voice that she was nervous. I wondered how Joan had told her about me. Was Joan there with her now?

It turns out she wasn't. There had been another change in plans, and Joan had decided that the whole ordeal was dragging on too long, so she had given my birth mother a call and told her everything. I would give anything to have listened in on that conversation.

"How are you?" were the first words I remember saying to my birth mother. A stupid question to ask a woman who has just been told that the child she placed for adoption thirty-two years ago has just resurfaced. How did I expect her to be?

If only I had taped our first conversation. I'd be able to replay it word for word. Unfortunately, I didn't tape it, and I can't remember the exact words we spoke.

I can see the scene being played over again and again, without sound. There I was, standing in the kitchen, pacing back and forth as I tried to make some intelligent conversation with my birth mother.

The only thing I can remember her saying is how sorry she was.

"You don't have to be sorry," I think I told her. "I don't blame you for anything."

"I always wanted to look for you," she said between sobs.

I didn't want her to cry.

"You must think I'm a bad woman."

"I never thought that for a moment."

"Do you think you can ever forgive me?"

If forgiveness was all she asked, I had no problem with that. I could easily forgive her, even though there was nothing to forgive. She had chosen to do what she had done because she really had had no choice.

"Of course I forgive you."

"I want to meet you," she told me. "If you want to meet me, that is."

"I'd love to meet you."

"I'm going to come up as soon as possible. I have a lot of vacation time coming to me. I can't come this week, but would next week be all right?"

"Anytime."

"Was it hard to find me?" she asked.

"Once I got my records from the hospital, it only took me a few calls."

"What did the records say?"

"Not much really." I didn't want to get into all the details on the phone. "They did list you as Maureen Donahue."

"I know," she said softly.

I wanted to ask her questions about my birth father. I was hesitant, though.

"Does he know about me?" I asked, hoping she would know who "he" was.

"Yes."

"He's a salesman?"

"Your father isn't alive."

I was very disappointed to hear that. One of my hopes had been to talk to him and possibly meet him eventually.

Learning in the way I did that he had died, took some of the wind out of my sails. The line of questioning I had hoped to pursue with my birth mother was no longer a straight and narrow path, especially since I noted a certain hesitation in her voice when she mentioned my birth father.

I was so tempted to ask her more questions about him. What was he like? How old was he when he died? How did he die?

I had a lot of questions. I didn't ask any of them. I just said, "Oh," when she told me he was no longer alive. It wouldn't have been fair to ask her anything else. At least not then, because it was her turn to be the center of attention. His turn would come later, if she were willing to talk about him.

She might not want to remember him. Maybe his memory was too painful for her. He might have died in her memory long before he had actually died.

I remember feeling a sense of sadness about his death, though. It was as if he were dying all over again. It made me think about something else. I tried to imagine how I would have felt if my cousin or aunt had told me that my birth mother was dead when I first made contact with the Hamiltons. Would I have felt comfortable enough to ask them questions about her? Or would my search have ended there?

That's part of the dialectic facing an adoptee in search, because death is the one real obstacle in any adoptee's search for his or her missing links. It's the last thing any adoptee wants to think about, but so many of the adoptee stories I've read, especially about older individuals, are filled with the regret the adoptee feels on learning that his or her birth mother or father has died before there could be a chance to talk. It's understandable how defeating it would be for an adoptee to expend so much actual and emotional time in a search, only to learn that the person being sought had long since died.

There's an emotional bond that inextricably ties people together in spite of separations, and each adoptee is aware of that bond without knowing its nature, which can only be revealed in the course of a successful search. That bond required that I learn more about my birth father. It wasn't enough to know that he had died. I wanted to know more about the living man. I was grateful for the opportunities I was going to have to learn about my birth mother, but I felt cheated by my birth father's death. Although that might sound selfish, there was something about my birth father that I needed to know. I had this gut feeling about him, something that linked us even in his death.

I didn't say anything more about him to my birth mother. I had no choice but to wait for the right opportunity to talk to her about him. That is, if there were ever to be a right time. There very well might not be a right time. And if that were to be the case, I was going to have to be satisfied with the little I did know about him.

Death might have been on my mind when I spoke with my birth mother, but she was more concerned with the present, more interested in the future.

"I can't wait to see my grandchildren," she said, her voice sounding more alive. "Joan told me you have a little one."

"Nicholas is four months old," I told her, "Jeremy is almost two-and-a-half, and Jennifer just turned five in February."

"I can't wait to see them."

The change in her voice was dramatic. She was no longer thinking about the past; she was thinking about what the future had in store for her. My children were the common element, the safe ground for my birth mother and me. She was interested in learning all about them, and I was eager to tell her.

We ended our first conversation in less than twenty minutes. No sooner was I off the line, and even before I had a chance to talk with Patty, than the phone rang again. It was Joan.

"Were you surprised?" she asked.

"Shocked would be a better description."

"I had to do it that way. Too many other people knew about you. I didn't think it was fair for Mo to be the last one in the family to learn about you. I hope you're not mad at me."

"I have no reason to be mad. I always realized the first conversation was going to be filled with some awkward pauses."

"How do you think she sounded?"

"Nervous," I said. "How did she react when you

broke the news?''

''She cried, but there was something different about her crying. It was as if a big burden was taken off her shoulders.''

''I'm glad it worked out that way.''

''She wants to see you, doesn't she?''

''If everything works out, she'll be coming up next week.''

''I wish I could be there, but I think it would be better if Mo went by herself.''

''You're probably right,'' I said, trying to convince myself more than I was saying to agree with Joan.

''Did she,'' Joan began, hesitating between words, ''say anything at all about your father?''

''Other than that he died, she didn't really say anything.''

''Did you ask?''

''I didn't think it was the right time to begin asking a lot of questions.''

Joan more or less agreed with me on that point, although I could sense there was something she was trying to tell me. For some reason, she couldn't bring herself to say anything more.

After the conversation with Joan, my phone didn't stop ringing for the next two days. My birth mother must have called at least five times, each time only talking a few minutes. Each time trying to reassure herself that everything was going to be all right. I think she was afraid that I was going to reject her. And although she never put it into words, I could tell what she felt, so I tried to convince her I was not about to reject her. Nothing I could say was going to convince her, however. She was going to have to deal with it herself.

She seemed to be receptive to my existence, because she told me how she called almost everyone she knew to tell them all about me. Of course, after she talked to somebody, I would get a phone call from that person. In the two days following the call from my birth mother, I talked to aunts, uncles, and cousins.

The most moving call I received, though, was from my birth mother's mother, my "new" grandmother. She was not doing well. Her health had begun to deteriorate, and she had been in and out of the hospital several times for one thing or another. At that time, she was recovering from a hip operation. I was initially concerned about what effect my arrival was going to have on her. My greatest fear was that I would be the cause of a setback in her recovery.

Before I talked with my grandmother, Virginia had dismissed my fears by telling me I had nothing to worry about. In fact, ever since my arrival into the family, my grandmother had taken a turn for the better. When I finally did get a chance to talk with my grandmother, she spent more than half our phone conversation crying. In between her tears, she managed to tell me how happy she was for her daughter. She also told me how glad she was to have another grandchild. Had she known about me before? Maybe not, but she had had strong suspicions.

My Aunt Virginia later told me about a conversation she and her mother had had before my birth mother had contacted me. It seems Virginia was saying goodnight to her mother one evening, when, for no reason other than that Virginia had been making secretive phone calls, my grandmother stopped her as she was about to leave the room.

"Mo had a baby once," was all my grandmother said.

Virginia didn't know what to say. It was as if her mother had picked up on everything that was going on around her and had put it all together. Just by saying that, she had added to the growing evidence that my birth mother's secret was not really a secret after all.

And what about my parents? How did they react? Had I still kept my search from them?

No. Luckily, as soon as I had made contact with Joan, I had told them all about my search. And I say "luckily" because I wouldn't have wanted to tell them about locating my birth mother after I had made my first contact with her.

When I told my parents about my phone call from my birth mother, they were both fascinated with my story. They didn't feel threatened by my search. They didn't feel hurt, and they didn't think I had violated some unwritten code of ethics for adoptees.

I asked my mother if she had ever given any thought to my birth mother. She answered, "I never had time to really think about her. She was a stranger."

"She's no longer a stranger," I remarked. "She's likely to come up and visit Patty and me and the kids."

"That's great," my mother said. "When?"

"She's trying to see if she can come visit two weeks from now."

I wondered if my mother wanted to meet Mo. "Do you think you'd ever want to meet her?" I asked.

"Why not?" my mother replied without having to think twice about it.

Another hurdle safely passed, and one that I had been worried about ever since I had stepped off the curb at 50th Street and Eighth Avenue on my way to St. Clare's. There had been at that time no telling how my mother might have reacted to my adoption search. And even if she hadn't reacted negatively to the searching, how certain was I she'd react as positively to the finding and the meeting? It's one thing to react to something in theory. It's a totally different matter to have to react to theory when it becomes fact.

I was proud of the way my parents handled this delicate affair. They were totally supportive, and rather than keep my discovery a secret, they shared it with their friends. And how did their friends react? For the most part, they responded positively, because it was obvious to them that my parents were positive about my search. There were only one or two holdouts who thought what I had done was terrible. But knowing who those people were, I wasn't at all surprised about their reaction. In fact, I would have been more surprised if they had reacted any other way.

My mother took the few negative views in stride. She was never the type to worry about what other people might say. Some months later, she confided to me that she thought of my search as the unfolding of a good novel, and she was excited to be part of it. With so many secrets about my past now in the open, my mother grew as curious as I did about some of the other secrets.

"Do you know anything about your father?" my mother asked me after we had talked about Mo.

"All I can tell you, and all that I have to tell isn't very much, but his name was George, and he was a salesman."

"Was?"

"My mother picked up quickly on my use of the past tense.

"He died in 1952," I told her. "In a car accident."

"Do you think you'll find out anything more about him?"

"I hope so."

And I did hope, because I was making the mistake of creating my birth father in a mythical image and likeness. The little reality I had was not sufficient enough for me to see him clearly. If the truth be known, the little reality I had didn't meet my expectations. It was hard not to be able to think any longer that he was a man connected with the theater. I didn't want him to be a salesman. I didn't want him to be Willy Loman, the character in Arthur Miller's *Death of a Salesman*. I wanted him to be Frederick March, the actor who played Loman. I was not willing to accept the facts, because they didn't support my fantasy.

Looking back on it all, I have a better appreciation of my feelings about my birth father, but at the time, his very existence was shrouded in mystery. What little bits and pieces of information I did learn seemed to have a false ring. I couldn't help but think that people were hiding something from me. I imagined George Donahue, if that was his real name, was a married man with a family. I further imagined that he might have been married at the time of my birth. What I couldn't imagine was why no one was willing to talk about him.

My imagining ceased suddenly one afternoon, a few days before my birth mother's visit. I was at work when Aunt Joan called. She sounded troubled.

"I don't know how to tell you this, Vincent," she said.

"Tell me what?"

"It's about your father. There's something you should know about him before you meet your mother."

"Why?"

"Because I know you're going to have questions about him. And I know you're going to want to ask your mother, but I don't know if she'll be able to talk about him to you."

"I don't understand."

"How religious are you?" Joan asked me after a long pause.

"How religious am I?" I repeated.

I wondered what that had to do with anything. Surely it had to be relevant or my aunt wouldn't have asked me.

"I'm not a religious fanatic, if that's what you want to know. But I would consider myself fairly religious. And not just because I attend church on Sunday, but because I strongly believe in the existence of a loving and merciful God."

"Well," she said, "what I have to tell you just might shake your faith."

What could she tell me that would shake my faith? Even if my birth father had been a convicted mass murderer, it wouldn't have made that much of a difference.

"Whatever you have to say," I told her, "you can tell me."

"I don't want you to be shocked or scandalized, but . . ."

At that moment Joan took a deep breath. I waited for what I imagined to be the bad news.

"Vincent, your father was a priest."

CHAPTER EIGHT

Bless Me . . . Father?

"YOU'VE GOT TO be kidding."

"I'm serious."

"I can't believe it."

"You better start believing it, because it's the truth. Your father was a Catholic priest."

My initial reaction upon hearing the news was to laugh out loud. Not because I thought the latest bulletin was funny, but because the fact that my birth father was a priest was probably the last thing in the world I had expected Joan to tell me.

I finally understood all the mystery that had surrounded my birth father's identity. It all began to make sense. Every time I had made even the slightest reference to my birth father, the subject had quickly been changed to something much safer. And it hadn't only been Joan who'd been adept at switching the topic. It seemed everyone else in the family who knew about it stayed clear of the topic when I was around.

I could understand why. Joan and the rest of her family didn't know me well enough to know how I would react to learning that my birth father was a Catholic priest. But no matter how many times I told Joan I wasn't aghast at the news, I couldn't convince her I was telling the truth.

Catholics are raised to think of priests in a certain way. When you think of them as "Father," you might think of them in a paternalistic way, but you'd never think of one as being a father as in "father and son." In my wildest imagination, I never had thought my birth father was a "Father" with a capital "F." Things like that only happened in epic novels or in television miniseries, not in real life. Or so I thought.

"So, you aren't going to hang up on me and tell me you want nothing to do with the Hamiltons anymore," Joan finally said, sounding somewhat reassured.

"Not at all. In fact, I find the whole thing amusing."

"Amusing? Here I was so afraid to tell you about your father, because I wasn't sure how you'd take the news, and you find it amusing. I don't understand."

"Don't take me wrong. I'm not trying to make light of it. It's just that there's nothing I can do about who my birth parents were. What happened happened a long time ago. And for whatever reasons it happened, there's nothing I can do about it. I'm here. That's all that really matters."

"So that means you're not going to hold it against your mother?"

"What point would there be in that?" I explained to Joan. "I don't know enough of the facts to make any accurate judgments, and even if I did, I don't think I'd have the right to stand in judgment."

"You don't know how glad I am to hear that," Joan said. "It will make things so much easier when your mother does tell you. But you'll have to promise me you won't say anything to her about it. You'll have to let your mother tell you in her own way and in her own time.''

"I understand, and I'm glad you told me, because I know I was going to ask her questions about my birth father when I met her.''

"At least now you'll understand why your mother seems reluctant to talk about your father.''

Of course I understood. And I was glad that Joan confided in me. I knew I had to back off from the issue of my birth father until my birth mother felt comfortable enough to talk to me about him, which, I believed, was going to be a very difficult matter.

While I might have understood the situation a little better, I was curious as to how Joan knew who my father was and how long she had known his identity.

"Did you always know who my father was?''

"Remember how confused I was,'' Joan said, "when you first talked to me on the phone?''

"Yes, I remember.''

"Well, it didn't take me long to solve who you were, but I wasn't sure right away who your father was. For awhile I was certain that your father and your half-brother or sister's father were one and the same. Somehow, after thinking about it some, I had my doubts.''

"What caused you to doubt it?''

"It was a feeling I had. Then when I talked to Virginia about it, she confirmed my suspicions about who your father was, and he isn't the same man who fathered the other child.''

"Did you know my father?''

"We all knew him. He was a very popular priest. There wasn't a woman in the parish who didn't have a crush on Father Pat.''

''Father Pat?''

''Patrick. Father Patrick Kearney. That was his name.''

Hearing his name for the first time, I had a flashback to the moment when Mrs. Chin told me my birth mother's name was Maureen.

For some reason, hearing his name made him very real to me. He was no longer a stranger. He had taken on an identity that I could relate to.

Joan was very good in telling me as much as she could about him, even though it only amounted to a thumbnail sketch of the man. The full details would not become evident until after I talked to my birth mother about him, and even then, the portrait I would have of him would not be the full picture. It wouldn't be until a few years later that I would see my birth father in all his complexity.

But, for the moment, when Joan opened the door that led into my birth father's real life, I was more than satisfied with what I was told.

His vocation was a matter for further digestion and contemplation. What I absorbed immediately was the knowledge that, in addition to his being a priest, Father Pat was also a writer. It turned out that Father Pat wrote for a Catholic radio show and did some ghost writing for Cardinal Spellman. He also taught English and drama at a Catholic high school for boys.

Joan told me that a well-known television and film star had been one of my birth father's students. ''In fact, if my memory serves me,'' she said, ''the year your father died, the school faculty presented that actor a drama award in your father's memory.''

I was impressed. I had always considered this film star a fine actor and a fine man. The fact that my birth father had any connection with him was a vicarious source of pride for me.

My head was spinning wildly when I finished talking with Joan. On one level, nothing was really changed. On another level, though, everything was different. Suddenly, dozens of adoption stories that I had read over the years came back to me in flashes of revitalized recognition. All the stories I had read about adoptees who after completing a search, learned that they shared something in common with a birth parent, made me re-think my position on heredity.

Before learning about my birth father, I had been more or less skeptical about inheriting talents. I thought the adoptee stories I had read about shared talents were mostly coincidental. I was less sure about that after talking with Joan.

There was a certain irony about my birth father's story that was both telling and a bit bizarre. I claimed to be a writer. It was the one thing I did that I had always wanted to do. It was the one calling that consumed me. Especially where the stage was concerned, because that's where both my heart and soul were—in the theater.

Even though the childhood fantasy I had had about my birth parents working in the theater hadn't come true, learning about my birth father's love for the theater and his involvement in it was enough to make me still believe in fairy tales. There was a connection there, but a connection that went deeper than a shared love for writing and the theater. It was something about his vocation.

As a young man, I had visions of one day becoming a priest. I actually thought I had a vocation. I imagined I could hear the call to serve God as a priest. In time, though the call persisted, the message was not as clear. I was getting mixed signals. There was something about the religious life that I found inviting, but I wanted to be assured that the invitation was really in my name and not just addressed to "occupant."

In reality, I was torn between two loves. By the time I had reached college, I still wasn't sure which direction to take. I had always felt I was at a crossroads. I always wondered if I was making the right decision. Ironically, I had used this conflict as a motivation for a play I had written. I had completed it just before I started my adoption search.

My play was called *Wishful Thinking*, and it was the story of a young man who had elected to join a cloistered Order of monks. Only a few months before he was to take his final vows, he heard a voice which told him his vocation was a mistake and that if he really wanted to do God's work, he would leave the Order and seek his true vocation.

Tim, the young man in my play, had always dreamt of becoming a Broadway playwright. His voice told him to go to New York and make a name for himself on the Great White Way. Tim hesitated. He didn't want to make a decision, because he needed some guarantee that, if he did leave the Order, he wouldn't be making a mistake.

His voice told him, "If you want guarantees in life, buy yourself a Timex watch. But if it's happiness and true contentment you seek, you have to be willing to take some risks." Tim struck a bargain with his voice.

He agreed to leave the Order on condition that if things didn't work out in New York in six months, he would be allowed to return to the Abbey.

Wishful Thinking was, when I wrote it, partly my story. It was also my birth father's story, because I was sure he, too, had been torn between two vocations.

The fact that I began my search after completing the play made my discovery all the more ironic. And it just wasn't that one play that made me think there was something to the link I had found. I had written the draft of another play in which a woman's path crosses that of a man—a priest—she had known when she was younger.

In that play, I dealt with the relationship between the woman and the man, and it was only at the end that the woman revealed the fact that the child she had given birth to was actually the priest's son.

Could it have been that I had a preoccupation with plays that were priestly, or did I just find illicit relationships a good source for drama? If there was some subconscious stream flowing through my psyche, I was unaware of it. But that doesn't rule out the possibility that a person may be more in tune with his or her life flow than he or she may realize. Call it coincidence, but I was hard pressed to believe that all the missing links in my life were merely coincidental.

There was something about my search that was bigger than just my desire to find my missing links. I was convinced, after talking to Joan that afternoon, that my search was for a purpose or to a purpose that was bigger than the one I had called my own. As the story began to unfold, bit by careful bit, the shadings and subtext were building to a great crescendo. Just when I had thought I had conquered Mount Everest, another peak appeared on the horizon.

In the beginning, when my search was mere speculation, I had thought my actual seeking would be on the straight and narrow. Instead, the path was far from straight. It had turned into a stream and had begun to ebb and flow like a river toward the sea. That river was clearly deceptive. On the surface was the simple task of locating my missing links. Below the surface was a far more complex task, because the missing links were not just those of my birth mother's and father's lives. Those submerged links were timeless, and I was new in the process of taking up and examining, of connecting certain bonds that existed despite my adoption.

Ironically, from the start of my search, it was my birth mother who dominated the landscape, and she still remained the larger figure in the overall picture, even after my birth father's identity became known to me. But it was my birth father who had suddenly become this mysterious force, a magnet that turned my head around. We were kindred spirits. There was a link that superseded any biological links. He was act one; I was act two. I followed him after a long intermission.

I believed he had passed on to me certain "God-given" talents, but at the same time, I realized that those talents were raw materials. I had to give my adoptive parents credit for providing some of the shaping and forming that had gone on in my life.

My search was not a matter of separating the wheat from the chaff. On the contrary, it was the sifting and blending of all the ingredients that would eventually yield a bountiful crop. I didn't know that then. At that particular moment in my life and in my search, I was on a plateau, not at the ultimate peak. My search was still in the process of moving forward. The best, or worst, was yet to come. The greatest challenge was the one that awaited me at Washington's National Airport. I would meet my birth mother for the first time. And even though there would be just the two of us, my birth father's ghost would have to be reckoned with when the time was right.

CHAPTER NINE

Moments in Time

MOMENTS BEFORE THE first passenger stepped off the plane that had carried my birth mother to Washington, I glanced over my shoulder, and from the corner of my eye, I saw three priests standing at an Avis counter, joking and showing their high spirits in all their movements and gestures. Ordinarily, I wouldn't have made a mental note of the scene, but now the presence of the priests became a painful reminder of the expression "in the wrong place at the wrong time."

Whether I was overreacting to the situation or not, I broke out in a cold sweat as I observed the priests filling out their car rental forms. If they were still standing there when my birth mother got off the plane, how was it going to look to her? I'm sure she had "priest" on her mind as much as I did, because when you want to avoid a subject, all you can think of is that subject.

Even if I had moved away from the Avis counter, my birth mother would have seen the priests, because they stood in the direct line of vision of the deplaning passengers. And since she would be scanning the arrival area looking for me, she was bound to see the three cavorting clerics.

As my deodorant went into overtime, the passengers began filing out of the plane. One by one. And the priests were still standing there. They were now arguing over what size car to rent. One of them, apparently the money-minded one of the three, wanted the smallest and least expensive car. The other two, both of whom were carrying expensive-looking golf clubs, wanted a car large enough to hold their luggage and clubs. In the end, which I never thought was going to come, the duffer priests won out and the trio, who had begun to remind me of the three witches in *Macbeth*, made their exit. And none too soon either, because it was only a matter of seconds before I noticed a woman who had to be my birth mother emerging from the exit door.

A casual observer never would have guessed at the magnitude of this reunion between a son and his birth mother, because it was so low-keyed, so completely devoid of drama. She didn't rush at me across the arrival area, her arms open wide waiting for my embrace. And I didn't plow over any unsuspecting pedestrians in an attempt to greet her. Instead, we greeted each other with our eyes. Each acknowledged the other's identity with a small smile.

It was obvious to me from the outset that my birth mother was a very private individual. Her body language registered low on the effusion scale. She was no Sophie Tucker. She was more like Mary Pickford. When I saw her, impeccably dressed in a white business suit, I can remember thinking she looked a lot younger than I had thought she would.

Other than cordial "Hellos," I can't, for the life of me, remember the exact words we exchanged at that moment. And I can't even begin to recreate the dialogue that might have been, because the words wouldn't ring true; they would merely be the words as I would like to remember our having said them.

Suffice it to say, we were both relatively tongue-tied. Both of us came to the airport with many preconceived notions, many fabricated fantasies, and with many hopes and wishes to be fulfilled. Since we were on my turf, since I was the "offensive" player, I was more relaxed and more in control than my birth mother. She was nervous. She couldn't find her baggage claim check at first, but after a frantic look through her pockets and purse, she found it, and nervously handed it to the agent as I picked up her luggage.

We didn't say much to each other as we made our way out of the terminal to the shuttle bus. Our conversation didn't amount to much more than small talk.

"How was your flight?" I asked.

"I thought we were going to be delayed," she answered, "but we made up for lost time in the air."

She didn't look anything like her sister Joan.

"Did you eat on the plane?"

"They had a nice cold lunch. I wasn't very hungry."

I tried to imagine what she had looked like when she was younger.

"Patty's having chicken for dinner."

"That's nice," she said.

Later on, I learned how much she hated chicken.

Small talk. Small things. Small pleasures and small measures of getting to know her, getting to feel free and easy. Getting to like her, getting to hope she liked me. It was an odd experience. We knew very little about each other. Likes and dislikes. Dreams. Desires. Favorite colors. Favorite books.

I liked to read. She didn't read much.

She was a Ronald Reagan fan, had always been one, even before he entered politics. She even had an autographed picture of him.

I loved the theater. She hadn't been to a play in years. But, in her youth, when she still was working in New York, she used to love to go to the theater and the famous night clubs.

So much to learn. So much to talk about. But how do you begin a conversation that has a thirty-two year gap?

And what had that gap done to my birth mother's perceptions? Was she the same woman she had been when she gave birth to me? Not likely. We all change. We all grow. Or do we? Some of us regress. Retreat into our own hand-crafted worlds—where there is a lie, where there is denial, where there is little chance for real growth.

How much did the lie—my birth mother's cover-up—get in the way of her growth? It was a difficult assessment to make, and one which could only be made, not on the spot, but over a period of time.

As my birth mother and I talked, I couldn't help but be distracted by my own thoughts. I was trying to imagine what was going through her mind as she talked to me. Whom did she see when she looked at me? Did she see a long line of Hamiltons? Was she trying to resurrect a memory or reconstruct some of her own missing links? Did I remind her of anyone in particular in her family, or was I a reflection of my birth father? And if I was his image and likeness, what effect did it have upon her?

Funny, my birth father might have been dead and buried, but he was riding in the car with us that afternoon, and his spirit was at work, because no sooner had I entered I-95 heading toward Fredericksburg, than my birth mother looked over and said, ''You know about your father.'' It wasn't a question. It was a statement looking for verification.

What was I going to do? Lie to my birth mother only minutes after meeting her? Was I supposed to feign ignorance and then act surprised when she told me? And what if she told me my birth father was the salesman he was supposed to have been? Should I take the safe way out and let the white lie continue to live?

That would be dishonest in more ways than one. I opted to be obtuse.

''Yes,'' I said. ''I think I know about him.''

I didn't say I knew he was a priest. I merely said, ''I think I know.'' It was up to my birth mother to interpret my response.

When she countered with, ''You don't think that makes me an evil woman, do you?'' I knew we were both using the same unspoken language, or why else would she have made that remark? If she hadn't thought I knew the ''truth,'' if she thought I was still under the impression that my father was the late George Donahue, salesman par excellence, there would have been no reason for her to ask me if I believed her ''evil,'' or some words to that effect.

''I wasn't sure how I was going to tell you.'' She looked straight ahead as she talked. ''It was the one thing I didn't want you to know.''

''Would it make a difference if I told you it didn't matter?'' I asked her, hoping she would understand that, although who my birth father was might have mattered, her relationship with a priest was not going to make a difference in our relationship.

She nodded her head.

And that was that. We had communicated via intimation. She knew that I knew. I knew that she knew I knew. Together we had begun to conquer the "lie" and to build a foundation based on truth.

The fact that my birth mother was able to bring up the subject of my birth father so soon after we met was an indication that she wanted the truth to come out.

I was a fairly good judge of character, and from the little I could observe, my birth mother was an emotional Hoover Dam. She must have crafted her emotional defenses until they had become a practiced art form. She talked about this and that, but she was only marginally willing to reveal the pain and heartache she had endured over the years. Denial had become a way of life. She had avoided dealing with the truth for so many years that she had created her own emotional reality. It was obvious, however, that there was some truth still working within her or she wouldn't ever have agreed to meet me.

Who was I to her? She was "mother" and I was "son" only in strict definition of the words. The biological link was only a thread. There was a need to find a foundation upon which a new relationship could be built.

The degree to which that relationship would grow would depend upon the open lines of communication we might establish. Miracles were out of the question. We weren't talking Hollywood. We were talking Fredericksburg. Reality. Flesh and blood.

Too many things had happened in my birth mother's life because of and in spite of her situation to make our relationship trouble-free. She was the one who had had to endure the full knowledge of her deeds. She was the one who had had to build a life based upon suffered consequences.

I had only had to grow up adopted. I had not had to endure anything but the wondering. My birth mother had had to suffer indignities as well as the added measure of wondering, but hers was a wondering on the opposite end of the spectrum from mine. How long, I found myself wondering, had it taken before she could look at another child and not think about the child she had given up? How long had it taken her to be able to rid her mind of the memory of briefly being a mother? When had she stopped wondering about where I was, and what I was doing?

I had to be careful. My wondering couldn't stay wondering very long, because the person I had been seeking, the person with all the answers, had been found. And with her sitting next to me, I could barely keep from unleashing a torrent of questions aimed in her direction.

Our conversation on the drive to Fredericksburg did not get to the heart of the matter. Instead of tackling the meatier subjects I had in mind, we talked mostly about my children. It wasn't only a safe topic; it was also a subject that miraculously animated my birth mother.

She was in the driver's seat. She had the questions, and I held the answers. She wanted to know everything about her grandchildren. It was as if she were cramming for her grandmother's exam.

Although it was a disappointment that I learned very little about my birth mother during our first hour and a half together, that misfortune was minor. It wasn't until that night, after the kids were in bed, that she and I got a chance to talk.

She was thrilled to have met her grandchildren. She was especially excited about Nicholas, because he was only four months old at the time. Jennifer was going on five, and Jeremy was nearly two-and-a-half. And while those two were still young, Nicky was a baby, and that meant a great deal to my birth mother.

While she was holding him, I came to understand something. Nicholas was actually me. He was the child she had left behind, not the thirty-two-year-old man I had become. He was the unconscious link she had been looking for. If anything, I was more the man she had left behind. I had been transformed into my birth father.

How odd, I thought. Here she has both the child she had to give up and the man she lost, all in one place and all at one time.

It was one of those revealing glimpses into the human condition that make life so fragile and genuine. And though we never talked about the transformation of personalities, I think we both understood what had happened.

With the ice not quite broken, merely cracked a little, my birth mother began to talk more about her family and her family relationships. I quickly learned that she was very close to her nephew Ted, the cousin born less than two weeks after I was born.

It was only natural that my birth mother would allow her maternal instincts to be nurtured on her nephew. It was understandable how she would, unconsciously, satisfy the feelings of loss for her son with the closeness of her nephew. For lack of her own child, she substituted my cousin for me. And in a way that was good, for her loss was softened somewhat, because she was able to shower her affection on a child.

In another way, it was not so good, because my birth mother would have a constant reminder of me—what my growing up might be—in my cousin. His first tooth. His first words. His first steps. All of them were my firsts, too.

She only had to look at him to see me.

Now that she had the real me, I wondered how I compared with my cousin. Had my birth mother created an image of me based on the reality of Ted? Did she expect me to live up to his personal legacy? In a way I think she did expect me to measure up to Ted, because over the course of years he had become the real thing, and I had become the substitute.

Thirty-two years later, the substitute shows up to claim his (rightful) place. But, what was that place, I wondered, and what right did I have to claim it? I was my birth mother's son, and nothing could change that; however, my cousin had grown in my birth mother's heart. A close relationship had developed between them. Ted, I learned later, had always considered Aunt Mo his "other mother." The bond that existed between Ted and my birth mother was something that my presence would never change and should never change. I didn't want to become guilty of alienating anyone's affections.

Before I ever got the chance to meet Ted, I talked to him on the phone. He was a very likable person, and in many ways, we did have things in common. He didn't have to tell me how much he loved my birth mother. I could tell by the way he talked about her. And for that I was glad, because although she might have been deprived of her child, she hadn't been deprived of a child's love.

Even my birth father figured in the story of Cousin Teddy and his Aunt Mo. That first night my birth mother showed me a picture of Ted's christening, and I couldn't help but be struck by the irony of the event. There she was holding Ted in her arms, and there was my birth father performing the baptism. What must have been going on in their minds?

"It was very difficult," she told me as she explained the scene. "I was very depressed after that. I didn't want to go on."

She put the picture back in her pocketbook and lit a cigarette.

"Your father was a very good man. He was a great priest, too. He could deliver a great sermon. His masses were always crowded. He was a wonderful writer. He always loved the theater, just like you."

As my birth mother sat across from Patty and me at the kitchen table talking about my birth father, I could hear that something extra in her voice. She wasn't talking about a man who had been dead since 1952; she was talking about a man who was still very much alive to her, very much a part of her life even in 1981. Seeing how she had opened up the subject, I took the risk of asking her some questions about my birth father.

"Where was he when I was born?"

"He was out of town."

"How did you tell him I had been born?"

"I sent him a telegram."

"A telegram!" I said, amazed that she'd take the chance of letting the world in on her secret.

"Of course I didn't come out and say he had just become a father."

"What did you say?"

"The telegram said, 'The package arrived safely.' "

I laughed. It had been a clever way to tell him.

"You should have said, 'The blue package arrived safely.' That way he would have known it was a boy."

It was her turn to laugh.

Her laughter turned solemn again when she told me how it was when she had to give me up.

"Since the hospital staff assumed I was a married woman, I left the hospital a free woman and a new mother. Little did they know where I was really going when I left. I had to get a taxi and be driven over to the Foundling Home across town. It was the longest taxi ride I ever had to take."

She paused to light another cigarette.

"I did some volunteer work at the Foundling Home after that. I worked in the nursery."

"Was I still at the Foundling when you worked there?" I was curious to know if she had gone there to keep an eye on me, or whether she just needed to have some physical contact with babies in general.

"No," she said, "you weren't there when I was."

Her answer was a disappointment. I had hoped she could shed some light on the missing links in my first few months of life. When I told her about the letter I had initially received from the Foundling, informing me there was no record of where I had been for three months, she seemed, from everything I could gather, confused by that fact. She claimed she had no idea why I hadn't been at the Foundling between the time she brought me there and the date my parents brought me home. I had no reason to doubt her claim, but there was something about the way she reacted that puzzled me. It was a reaction that I would see repeated often when we were together, and I would either ask certain questions or recount events as I knew them, and hope she would supply the missing information.

Her responses seemed conditional, and her reactions appeared to be delayed, as if she were not reacting so much to what I was telling her, as to something she already knew, something she had locked away in the recesses of her memory.

I think she knew more than she was willing to tell me. I think I might have been moving too fast, covering too much ground, opening up too many wounds.

My birth mother needed time to accept the fact that I was not going to reject her because of something she might tell me. She was deathly afraid of telling me anything that might have made me change my opinion about locating her. Even though I tried to tell her, in both words and deeds, that the past didn't matter, I was contradicting myself, because I persisted in wanting to know all about what had happened.

Unfortunately, she couldn't yet understand the difference between my wanting to know what had happened in the past and what seemed to her my search for evidence to make accusations against her. The years of denial had finally caught up with her. Before I came along, there had been no one who could challenge her with questions. All her denials stood firm and became granite monuments which I began to chisel away with my questions.

When I saw that she was exhausted from my questions, I backed off and let the rest of our first weekend together proceed in the present tense. She talked more about her family and about the people she worked with. From the way she talked about her job, I could tell her career meant everything to her.

She was a workaholic. She worked six days a week and brought work home with her for Sunday. She rarely took off work, even losing vacation time, rather than leave the office for a few days. And what little vacation time she did take, she would spend making obligatory trips to her family.

There were no real friends in her life. No people she shared any time with. She seemed to have neglected her personal life for a conventional business career.

I couldn't help but be reminded of the line from Robert Frost's "Mending Wall" in which he talks about not knowing whether you're walling something in or walling something out. In an attempt to wall in her past, my birth mother was walling out people who could have made a real difference in her life. Now for better or worse, that wall was no longer impenetrable. There were a select few non-family members whom she wanted—needed—to tell all about me and who I was.

I don't know if she was aware of it or not, but there was a certain cleansing effect her new "open admissions" policy had on her. The more people she was able to tell about me, the more she was able to penetrate that wall of silence that had enclosed her and kept her engulfed in her own past.

The fact that my birth mother's personal admissions were not met with shock and dismay couldn't have been more therapeutic. She needed to realize, however, that it was going to take more than a score of "mea culpas" to free her totally from the cocoon of self-inflicted guilt. She was merely a starting point, not the finish line. She, as well as I, had many more miles to go in our effort to untangle some unfinished business.

And topping the list of business tasks needing attention was the matter of my sibling, her first child. I didn't want our first weekend to end before I had at least broached the subject. I needed to know where we stood. But how was I to bring it up without causing her to retreat behind her wall?

The solution came coincidentally when my birth mother asked to see the documents I had found at St. Clare's. I, of course, knew what was on the documents, because I had committed the details to memory, but my knowledge of them was not at issue. The question was, did my birth mother know what was on the records? Or had she forgotten? Or, then again, had she remembered but needed to verify her memory?

The answer, I think, was yes to all of the above. The records from St. Clare's were only of minor importance to my birth mother, because she knew she would eventually have to get around to addressing the subject of her first child.

Feeling somewhat awkward, I made some excuse to leave the room while she looked over the crucial birth records. When I came back in, she had put the records back on the coffee table across the room.

"I guess you know," was what I remember her saying.

"You don't have to talk about it . . . now. It can wait," I said.

I wanted to allow her to tell me about it in her own time, but she needed to get it over with.

"You didn't have the same father," she told me. I

could tell she assumed I already knew.

I nodded my head.

She took a long drag on her cigarette. Her hands began to shake a little.

"He was a priest."

I tried to keep my face from registering the combined shock and surprise I felt when she told me my half-brother's or sister's birth father was also a priest.

"I sure knew how to pick them," she said before I could make any sensible response.

None of the questions I had seemed appropriate at the time, so I decided to remain silent. I just hoped that she would be willing to say more.

"He and your father knew each other. They were good friends."

That really didn't explain my birth mother's relationship to them. In fact, it confused the matter even more. Just when I thought I had it all straightened out in my mind, she destroyed my simplistic theory. I had imagined that she had been made pregnant by a layman and had sought counselling from my birth father.

I wanted to know how it had happened, but I didn't ask, because I didn't think it was my place to ask her about how she had managed to have a child by the first priest when I hadn't even dared to ask how she had managed to have a child with my own birth father.

Only after a long drawn-out listening session, did I have a somewhat clearer picture of my birth mother's past relationship with the clergy. I didn't learn how she came to start a relationship with the first priest, Father Francis Stepler, but I did come away from our talk knowing that that relationship had soured immediately after she became pregnant. He dropped her and wanted nothing more to do with her after that.

She showed a certain amount of anger, even moderated rage, when she talked about this man. As a parish priest he might have been all things to all parishioners, but to my birth mother he was a scoundrel. Obviously, there had been no way she could keep her first baby. She had had to place the child for adoption.

All she was willing to tell me about the child was that it was a boy. A boy who, according to my birth records, was two years old when I was born.

When I asked her if she knew what had happened to him, she told me she had no idea where he had gone, though she had been sent a picture of him when he was about a year old.

Any hope I had of seeing that picture was dashed when she told me she had torn it up right after receiving it in the mail.

"Why?" I asked her.

"I wanted to forget all about it. I didn't want to know anything."

"What if he ever contacted you?"

I couldn't tell from her reaction to my question if the thought had ever crossed her mind. I tried to tell her that there was as much chance of his one day locating her as there had been of my locating her. She didn't want to discuss it. As far as she was concerned, it was a closed subject, and not because she had any ill feelings about her first child, but because she had never come to terms with her relationship with his birth father.

It was different with my birth father. He didn't abandon her in her hours of need. He stayed by her, and I think he must have loved her. Or so I thought at the time. There was such a difference in my birth mother's tone of voice when she talked about my birth father. After all those years, she sounded like a woman in love.

And when she told me about my father's death, I could sense that she had mourned the loss of the greatest love in her life . . . not just when it happened, but over and over again.

By the end of the long evening, I was emotionally exhausted. By the end of the weekend, my birth mother was physically exhausted, because she wasn't accustomed to the high energy level of little children.

After retracing my steps to National Airport the Sunday evening of her departure, I had a great deal to think about, a great amount of information to sort out.

All in all, I would have to say it was a very good first meeting. When we dropped my birth mother off at the airport, both Patty and I realized there was still a need for more time. Time for my birth mother and me to get to know each other. Time to feel comfortable enough to talk openly and honestly.

It wouldn't happen overnight. It wouldn't all be resolved in the next visit. It would take much more time than that to unravel thirty-two years of lost, strayed, and stolen moments.

CHAPTER TEN

Time . . . Heals Everything?

MY BIRTH MOTHER began an independent campaign to become the sole support of the telephone company by running up a phone bill of more than $400 between late March and mid-April. She called me on the average of once each weekday, and at least twice a day on the weekends. There was little new ground covered in our conversations. Most of the talk was of the small variety, but it served as a form of therapy for her.

She feared rejection. She couldn't believe that I wasn't going to tell her to go away and get out of my life. Each time she called, I had to reassure her that I was not going to do that. And although she said she believed me, she still needed constant convincing.

During one of our conversations, a few days before Good Friday 1981, I told her my parents would be coming down from New York to spend Easter at my house. She never mentioned anything to me about wanting to be there too, and I never thought of inviting her, because she had just been to visit for the first time only a few days earlier. I just assumed she couldn't afford to make another trip that soon.

Money was not the issue, I was to learn after I got a call from my sister that same night. It seems my birth mother had phoned my sister. It wasn't the first time they had talked. This time my birth mother had mentioned Easter at my house without coming out and saying she either wanted to come up or expected to be invited. My sister could tell from the evasive way she was talking about it, however, that she really wanted to come up for the Easter weekend, but was afraid to come right out and ask me.

"I think you should call and ask if she'd like to come up for Easter," my sister said.

"You would think she might have said something about it to me," I replied, "especially since I told her it was too bad she hadn't planned her first visit around Easter. She agreed with me but she never even hinted that she wanted to come up."

"What if you had invited her?"

"I didn't want to make her feel obligated. I didn't want her to think she had to say yes just because I invited her."

"What if you made plane reservations for her and then called her and told her?"

"It's worth a shot," I said.

And that's what I did. I called the airline and made a reservation for her to come up the day before Good Friday. If I called her and she told me she couldn't come, I'd simply cancel her reservation and that would be the end of the matter.

"I just made a reservation for you to come up and visit for Easter," I told her on the phone, not knowing how she'd react.

"Wait a minute," she told me. "Let me get a pencil and a piece of paper so I can take down the reservation number."

I didn't have to twist her arm. I did, however,

have to plan for that first meeting between my birth mother and my mother.

Although they had talked to each other on the phone, they had not yet met. I began to wonder what that first meeting was to be like. Would they be nervous? Would they like each other? Did they have to like each other?

Fortunately, my mother was an easy person to meet. She was unassuming. She didn't have a threatening bone in her body. She had accepted my birth mother in theory, so I had no worry that she wouldn't accept her in practice.

When it came time for me to make that first introduction, I was probably more nervous than either my mother or my birth mother. Because neither of them was a garrulous person, their initial meeting was subdued and low-keyed. I opted to excuse myself after making the introductions, to allow these two mothers to talk in private.

When I looked back in on them a half-hour later, they were quietly chatting as if they had known each other for years. Jennifer and Jeremy were sitting at my mother's feet coloring in the new coloring books she had given them, and Nicholas was sitting in my birth mother's lap. Whether they were to become fast friends was something for the future. What really mattered was that they had solidified another link in the adoption story.

My mother assured my birth mother that she had never harbored any ill feelings toward her. My birth mother thanked my mother for being the woman who raised me. Perhaps it was the dramatist in me, but I couldn't overlook the dual symbolism of the time of year at the meeting of these two women. Theologically, it was the time of the resurrection—a time of rebirth. Seasonally, the world was in full bloom, with gardens of colorful tulips and other early spring flowers decorating the landscape. It was the most appropriate time of year for my two mothers to meet. A time for a rebirth, an affirmation of the life cycle and the importance of both giving birth and nurturing new life.

The spirit of Easter continued all that first spring, as I learned more about my birth mother and her family, and it culminated in August when Patty and I and our children attended a Hamilton family reunion in our honor. I met four generations of Hamiltons, aunts and uncles, cousins and the children—and my grandmother.

At 85 years of age, my grandmother was a frail but remarkable woman. It touched me to meet her, because in meeting her, I felt I was making direct contact with the past, and watching her with my children, I was also seeing into the future.

The joyous celebration was saddened by only one thing in the person of Arlene, my birth mother's youngest sister. Arlene was the only family member who had not been told about me. When she arrived at the party, she thought she was attending a family get-together. Little did she know that I was the guest of honor.

Arlene didn't know about me, because no one in the Hamilton family knew how to tell her that Maureen had had a child. Not that the news would have scandalized Arlene, but because it would have hit too close to home. When Arlene was an unmarried young girl, she became pregnant. My birth mother helped her through the ordeal and helped arrange for the child's placement and eventual adoption. Less than two years later, Arlene became pregnant again, but this time she couldn't bring herself to give up her child for adoption. Although she never married her son's father, he was given that father's last name.

Regrettably, that wasn't the end of Arlene's ordeal. Two years after the birth of her son, she gave birth to another child. Recognizing that she couldn't raise another baby without benefit of a husband, Arlene placed that child for adoption. A ray of happiness had entered Arlene's life when she married a man who was pleased to help her raise the only child she had been able to keep. Darkness shattered that simple happiness one afternoon in 1973 when Arlene's husband went to check on her son and found him on the floor, the victim of a drug overdose. As if that weren't tragedy enough, Arlene's husband was stricken with a fatal heart attack as he waited on the front stoop for the ambulance to come for her son. In that one afternoon Arlene lost the two people who meant most to her. That's why the family had found it too difficult to tell her about me. They didn't know how she would react to the reminder of her own losses.

When Arlene did arrive at the party, my birth mother greeted her and brought her over to meet me.

"Arlene, this is my son."

Probably not the most subtle introduction, but a start, anyway.

Arlene said "Hello," smiling as if nothing out of the ordinary had just happened.

"I'll talk to you later," she told me as she patted Jeremy on the head. "I want to go over and say hello to Bill."

As she walked away, I looked at Patty and Patty

looked at me. We were saying to each other with our eyes, "Is that all there is?"

To the uninitiated, it might have appeared to be all there was going to be on the subject, but a lot was happening behind the scenes. After Arlene talked to Bill, she pulled Joan aside and asked "who the hell" I was.

Joan filled her in on all the details, and from what Joan told me later, Arlene was thrilled for my birth mother. She didn't get around to saying anything to me about it, but she had planned to give me a call the following week or so to talk more about it.

A call did come less than two weeks after the family reunion, but from my birth mother, not from Arlene.

"Arlene died last night," she told me.

I was stunned and lost for words.

"How?"

"She fell in the bathroom while she was taking a shower. She hit her head on the edge of the tub. She had a serious concussion but didn't know how serious. Instead of going to the hospital to check it out, she told her boyfriend that she was going to take a nap. She never woke up."

Later, when I talked to Joan about Arlene's death, she told me that the day before she died, Arlene had talked to her about me. She was so glad for my birth mother. So glad that things had worked out so well for me. It gave her an added measure of faith that the two children she had placed for adoption had also been cared for and loved. She even hoped one day that I might have been able to help her locate her two children.

I am sorry I never had the chance to help her find her children. I think they would have been proud to know that their birth mother really did love them.

One day six months after Arlene's death, I got another urgent call from my birth mother.

"Nana's in the hospital. She had a heart attack. They don't expect her to live. I'm flying up to New York to be with her."

"I'll make arrangements at work to get up to New York tomorrow," I said. "I'll meet you at the hospital."

Fortunately, my grandmother made it through the next few days. It gave my birth mother and the rest of the Hamilton family a chance to say goodbye to her.

There was another one of those "I'll never forget" scenes at the hospital. My birth mother and I were in the intensive care unit where my grandmother was hooked up to miles of tubing which connected her to forbidding-looking medical equipment. She couldn't talk. She could barely keep her eyes open, but she did manage to make eye contact with me as I put my hand in her hand.

I didn't say anything to her. I just smiled at her as my birth mother talked to her. Before I took my hand away, my grandmother gave it the slightest little squeeze and spoke in a barely audible voice.

"I love you," was all she said.

Three days later, I joined the rest of the Hamilton family gathered to pay our final respects. The funeral mass was said by a priest who had once served the Hamiltons' parish, a priest who also happened to have been in the parish when my birth father was there.

My birth mother had told him all about me. I never was able to learn if the information really came to him as news, or if he just reacted with surprise for my mother's sake.

When I was introduced to him after the funeral mass, he took my hand and told me, "Your father was a wonderful man."

He gave my birth mother a big hug and a kiss. It was his way of telling her everything was all right.

Now, ask me if, when I first started my adoption search, I ever expected to become so interlinked with so many different people. I'd answer, not in my wildest imagining did I ever think I'd be going to family reunions and family funerals. I thought my search would be nothing more than making contact with a few key people. Little did I realize that it would not end so neatly or simply. There was much more I had to do before I could call my search complete. There were still many questions that were not resolved to my satisfaction.

One of the more immediate gaps concerned my birth father. He was too much of an enigma for me not to want to find the man behind the mystery. All I really knew about him was that he had been one of four children, another of whom was a nun in a teaching Order. Another of his sisters was a writer for a New York advertising agency.

Short of making direct contact with one of my birth father's relatives, I was at a loss as to how I might find and connect the missing links in that part of the chain. Again, my path to knowledge about my birth father revealed itself coincidentally. I just happened to have lunch one afternoon with a former high school teacher.

Sister Malachy was probably the best teacher anyone could ever have. She was wise, witty, and a real inspiration. When I told her the story of my search, I happened to mention the fact that my birth father's sister was also a nun teaching at a New York college.

"Do you remember Maggie Kearney?" she asked me.

"Of course I remember Maggie. We even dated a few times after we graduated from college. She went to Adelphi."

"Maggie's aunt, Mother Kearney, also teaches at a college in New York."

"Do you think it's possible we're talking about the same aunt?"

I had to find out. So that night I looked up Kearneys in the Nassau County phone book, hoping that Maggie's family still lived in the same town they had lived in when we were in high school. They didn't. And the only name that seemed vaguely possible turned out not to be a Kearney related to Maggie's family.

Never one to give up without a reasonable fight, I thought about another way of getting in touch with Maggie. In recollecting earlier details, I remembered that Maggie had gone to Adelphi with another graduate from our high school. If I could somehow locate Barbara, she might be able to tell me how I could locate Maggie.

Realizing that Barbara had married and had taken her husband's name, which I didn't know, I looked up Barbara's parents' number. Since Barbara and I had spent time working on the high school paper together and on some other projects, I had met her parents a few times. I could only hope that when I mentioned my name in connection with their daughter, they might remember who I was.

I called them, and they did recognize me. Barbara had moved to Westchester. I called her at her home and told her my story.

Minutes later, I was dialing Maggie's number in Minnesota. She was surprised to hear from me, and even more surprised when I told her my story. I asked if she thought there was a connection.

"Mother Kearney isn't my aunt. She is my father's cousin. Father Pat was also my father's cousin," she continued as she began tracing the Kearney family tree for me.

"I can't believe it," I told her. "Here you and I went to school together for four years, and we never knew we were related."

"If I were hearing the story about somebody else, I probably wouldn't believe it," she said.

When I asked Maggie what she might have remembered about Father Pat, she told me what she knew about him came mostly from the stories she had heard in her family.

"After he died, his family canonized him. His image and memory are sacred."

"How do you think they would take to the idea that he had a son?"

"I don't think Mother Kearney would be wild about the idea, but Father Pat's sister Eileen might be able to deal with it."

"What do you think I should do?"

"I think you have every right to call them, but if it would make things easier for you, I could call our fathers' mutual cousin, Betsy, and see what she thinks."

If Maggie had her way, Betsy was going to be another new character in my unfolding melodrama.

"Betsy," Maggie went on to explain before I had a chance to say anything, "is a really understanding person. If there's anybody in the Kearney family who would understand, Betsy would."

"It's worth a try," I told Maggie, making arrangements to call her the following week to see how her conversation with Betsy might turn out.

When I called her a week later, Maggie said the minute she got on the phone, "I have bad news for you! I couldn't believe the way Betsy reacted. You would have thought I had told her Father Pat was a wanted war criminal."

"It was that bad?"

"Bad," Maggie told me, "doesn't cover it. Betsy wanted to know what proof you had. I told her your birth mother told you about Father Pat. She then told me you'd have to have more proof than that if you were ever to contact any of Father Pat's family."

"Why do you think she reacted so negatively?"

"Like I told you, Father Pat has always been considered the Kearneys' own family saint, and here you come along, some stranger with this bizarre story that you're Father Pat's illegitimate son."

"Were those her exact words?" I asked.

"That's less of what she said than more, but I knew I had no chance of reasoning with Betsy the way she reacted. She didn't want to hear another word about it. I'm sorry."

"You have nothing to be sorry about. You did more than I could have expected."

"But it doesn't make sense. There's no reason why you can't meet the Kearneys and tell them who you are. God, if my mother has no problem accepting your story, I can't see why Father Pat's family can't."

"I don't think I'm ready to take that chance yet. The last thing I want to get involved in is some family

mess. I'm better off if I back off and forget about it."
And that's what I did. I made a decision after talking
with Maggie that I'd have to close the book on the
Kearney family. I couldn't bring myself to persist in
making direct contact, and that was a shame. A shame
for me and a shame for adoptees in general.

For the first time in my search, I knew what it
meant to feel unclean. I knew what it meant to feel rejected, even if that rejection came third-hand. It was one
thing to be told that the Kearney family wasn't prepared to meet with me. That I could understand. It
didn't take a genius to figure out that such news, especially as it related to a priest who had earned such a high
place of honor within his family, would be met with
some shock and disbelief. But only disbelief, not out-
right denial.

It was the denial that seemed to bother me most.
That they would find it hard to believe that their be-
loved Father Pat was a father in more ways than one
was something I was prepared for. I was willing to wait
for the family to digest the news before meeting me. I
was even willing to have only one of my birth father's
brothers or sisters be involved. It didn't have to be a
major production.

But to be told, as indirectly as it might have been,
that I was a liar and a fake was more than I was prepared to handle.

Proof? They needed proof? What more proof could
I give them than my birth mother's word? Why would
she have lied about such a thing? It would have made
more sense if she had kept her story about the salesman, George Donahue. At least, that would have made
more sense to me, had she wanted to perpetuate a lie.

But to admit willingly that she had had an affair with a priest, an affair that had resulted in her pregnancy, was to be brutally honest.

Well, it seemed that honesty, whether brutal or not, was not acceptable to the Kearney clan.

All hopes that I had had of unifying my missing links now had to be prematurely abandoned because of a third party's decision. Not that I couldn't have dismissed Betsy's warnings. I could easily have made a call to my birth father's sister Eileen, the sister who was the writer for an advertising agency. I could have called her, because I knew exactly where she lived, and in fact had looked up her phone number the week I had called Maggie.

I made my decision, however, not to do anything. Or at least, not to do anything then. I had to settle for what my search had netted me. I had to resign myself to the fact that whatever I was to learn about my birth father would have to be revealed by my birth mother.

It was a bittersweet pill to swallow, but I had learned that life was not always sweet to the taste. You had to take, as my mother used to tell me, ''the bitter with the better.''

CHAPTER ELEVEN

Time Flies. . . or Something About Building Rome

THERE'S SOMETHING TO the expression, "Rome wasn't built in a day," that seems applicable to my adoption search. When I was growing up, my mother often replied to my expressions of impatience with that statement. Whether I might have been frustrated by some trivial event or circumstance in my life, or whether some long-term dream or plan I had seemed to be blocked, my mother would remind me about Rome under construction.

"Remember, Vincent," she'd tell me, time and time again, "Rome wasn't built in a day. You have to be patient."

At first I didn't understand what the building of a city in Italy had to do with my childhood plight, but later on I grew to understand why my mother told me that and what it really meant to me.

Building a relationship is a lot like building Rome. It takes time and an inordinate amount of practice to build a solid relationship. I had to keep reminding myself of that fact when I considered the new relationship I had with my birth mother and her family.

The relationship I had, or was going to have, with my birth mother was not something that could develop overnight. There would have to be some give and take.

Some exploration of feelings. And there was definitely going to have to be some growth on both sides, because without mutual growth, a relationship is doomed to stagnate and finally die.

The only real obstacle in the way of the relationship that was forming between my birth mother and me was the variance of our individual perspectives. She wanted to have the family she had never had. She wanted a "picture-perfect" television family. And I can understand why. It was only natural for her to have fantasized about me as much as I had fantasized about her.

Where, in my mind, I had created the story of my birth parents, she had created her own story about her son. The success of any good story is often found in the casting. Get the right actors to play the parts, and your drama could become a smash hit. Miscast even one character, and you could spoil the entire dramatic effect. In my case, I can't say I was from central casting. I was not created out of "Father Knows Best." I was a married man with three children, trying to carve out a career and a life with some meaning in it. My birth mother was not the woman I had expected or invented. And by the same token, I was probably not the marble-chiseled son she had imagined. We were not living in a fairy tale. There were no sets, no costumes, and no special effects. What we saw was what we got.

Granted, I wished that my birth mother had been an energetic, outgoing ball of fire. I would have liked her to be a devil-may-care person with a great sense of humor. I wanted Mary Tyler Moore or Bea Arthur. Instead, my birth mother was more the mature Claudette Colbert or Nancy Reagan type . . . dignified and reserved.

128

Not that there's anything wrong with that type. What's wrong is requiring another person to live up to your expectations. I had to accept my mother on her terms as the person she had become. And she, in turn, had to accept me for the person I was. There was no room for fairy tales in our relationship. It had to be honest. It had to be real.

Unfortunately, it was a lot easier for me to be direct. I wasn't the one who had spent years covering up the truth about my youth. There were things in my birth mother's life that she alone could come to terms with, the most pressing of which was her pending retirement, which was the last thing she was looking forward to, even though she wasn't particularly thrilled with her job now. Her work filled up her waking hours; it was something to do to make the days shorter.

Although we had talked about what she planned to do when she stopped working, she had no real plans. She had thought she would continue working forever.

Forever came to an abrupt end when some office reorganizations forced my birth mother to choose between taking a retirement package or a job under a new boss. She reluctantly chose retirement, because she considered it the lesser of two evils.

In the beginning she had no problem with retirement. The beginning, however, was short-lived. Time became her enemy. She took a bad fall on the apartment grounds one afternoon and was laid up with an injured back for a few months.

And then she began drinking.

Not really "began" drinking, but she started to drink more than she had in the past. And her drinking was made all the worse, because I wasn't supposed to know she had a drinking problem, in fact had had one for many years. It was one of the things she wanted to keep from me. One of the blotches in her character she hoped I would not detect.

I knew about her problem almost from the beginning. I wasn't told about it, but I could sense it in her voice. There were far too many incoherent phone calls, far too many repeated stories for me not to know that she was an alcoholic. Knowing about a problem and doing something positive to solve it are two entirely different things. I was torn between doing what was kind and doing what was needed to set things right.

If I'd had an extra amount of courage, I would have talked to my birth mother about her drinking. It would have been difficult to confront her, not because I wanted to ignore her problem, or make believe it didn't exist. I thought by continuing our relationship, by encouraging her to live a healthy life for her new grandchildren and by just telling her I cared, I could lead her into moderation.

Although I hate to admit it, for several months I imagined that I had done the right thing. I had even imagined that her drinking problem was under control. I was wrong on a few counts. I was wrong to assume that if a person with a history of drinking didn't consume alcohol in my presence, such temperance meant the problem was under control. When my birth mother would visit us, she wouldn't have a drop of alcohol to drink, but because she was depriving herself of an occasional drink with us, it was that much harder on her, both physically and mentally, to abstain from drinking when she was alone. When she went home and had a few drinks, the sudden alcohol intake was too much for her system to tolerate.

At the time she was "forced" into retirement, she began to seek solace in increasing amounts of alcohol. So much so that I received a phone call one afternoon from Aunt Joan telling me that my birth mother was in the intensive care unit of a hospital in the city in which she lived. She had been admitted by her doctor for acute alcoholism, and while in the hospital, she somehow had fallen and been knocked unconscious.

I managed to take off from work for a few days, and I flew down to my birth mother's with Joan. When I arrived at the hospital with Joan, my birth mother's condition had worsened. There were two blood clots on her brain. Her liver had just about stopped functioning, and chest x-rays indicated that her lungs were in no better shape. As a few other family members gathered together at the hospital, the doctor told us that although the situation was not entirely hopeless, there was a very good chance that she might not make it through the week.

We held vigil at the hospital, each one of us with our own private thoughts. My cousin Ted and I had a chance to talk about my birth mother. He made clear to me again that he thought of her as a second mother.

As to my thoughts, I didn't have much of a past to fall back on. I could only think about the future and what life would be like for her if she did recover. It was obvious that my presence and the existence of grandchildren was not enough for her, at least not enough to change the destructive habits of many years' standing. There had to be something more in her life. She needed a reason to live, and that reason had to come from within her. It couldn't be supplied by a son or by a *dozen* grandchildren. I remember thinking how helpless I felt as we all sat in the intensive care waiting room. I felt helpless because I knew I didn't have the power to change her future, or even a notion of how to help her begin that change.

During the course of our extended vigil, my Aunt Virginia had a chance to talk to me about my adoption search. When the conversation moved around to my birth father, Virginia told me something about him that I had not learned before.

"Your father," Virginia said softly, "had another child."

I looked at her with total disbelief.

"It's true. Your father had a child by another woman in the parish. She was a married woman."

I didn't say anything. I couldn't believe what I was hearing. How was it possible? Not how could he have had another child by another woman, but how was it possible that my aunt knew about it? Could it have been just another one of those parish rumors?

"What did this woman do with the child?" I finally asked. "Did she place the baby for adoption?"

"No, she kept the baby and raised it in her family."

I don't remember if I asked Virginia if she knew whether the woman's husband knew about it, or whether the child was ever told about it. I guess I was in too much of a state of shock to ask any direct questions.

"How about that?" I wondered to myself. "Before I began my search, I always thought I was an 'only' child; now I find out I have two half-siblings."

That piece of information made me think more about my birth mother's other child and how much I wanted to find him. At least I knew there would be a slight chance of locating him, but this other sibling—my birth father's child? How in the world would I ever find him or her? Where would I begin? Place a personal ad in the church bulletin asking if the woman who had a child by Father Patrick Kearney would please contact me?

I was afraid of how many responses I would get. It might sound perverse to think that way, but I was beginning to wonder—if my birth father had fathered two known children, how many unknown children might there have been? As far as I knew, I might have had to rent out the Radio City Music Hall for a convention of my siblings!

Stranger things could happen. And so could miracles. Against all odds, my birth mother pulled through her illness and eventually after some weeks of hospitalization and some months of further recuperation at Virginia's home, she regained her strength and resumed a normal life.

Two years after her near death battle, she joined a ballroom dance class and began to enter dance shows and competitions. By that time she had also stopped drinking, which was the best stop of all.

Six fast and furious years quickly passed before I knew where they'd gone. Time had flown, and well, Rome was still under construction. I realized I had gone about as far as I could go with my birth mother in the continuing search for missing links. Our relationship excluded any more delving into the past.

My attempt to make contact with my birth father's family remained feeble at best. After years of denying myself the right to tell someone in that family who I was, I mustered up enough courage to call my birth father's unmarried sister Eileen, because I had become convinced—or at least I had convinced myself—that my birth father must have told someone in his family about me, and this unmarried sister seemed to be the logical choice. And if that were the case, there was no reason why I shouldn't be allowed to call and say "Hello."

I was so convinced, in fact, that I was a nervous wreck all over again making that first phone call, and I was as much a nervous wreck after the call, because it couldn't have turned out much worse.

Maggie had been right about the Kearney family. They were very protective of my birth father's memory. And even though his sister didn't deny the possibility that I was who I had claimed to be, she told me, in no uncertain words, that there was no chance in hell that she would ever be able to meet me.

I didn't like feeling like a "bastard." Whatever shame my existence might have invoked in other people, I was not ashamed of who I was and how I had come to be. My aunt might not have wanted to meet for a host of reasons, but I was determined that non-meeting was going to occur on my terms, not hers.

If she was going to reject me, it was only going to be after I had asserted my identity. And the best way I saw fit to do that was in a letter. A few months after my abortive phone call with my aunt, I followed it up with a letter. I told her that I could understand how she felt. I also told her that she was missing out on something by shutting me out.

I told her, in no uncertain terms of my own, that I was well worth getting to know, and if she didn't think so, it would be, unfortunately, her loss and not mine. I promised her I would never "darken her doorway," but, I said, even though we might never meet, it still didn't take anything away from the fact that I was her brother's son.

My aunt responded to my letter in a most warm and considerate fashion. In essence, she told me that too many years had elapsed since her brother was alive to allow her to start a relationship with me. Enclosed with the letter was a religious medal. She made no reference to the medal, but I could only assume, from the age of it, that it might once have belonged to my birth father.

The medal arrived shortly before my son Jeremy's first communion. I thought about giving it to him for his communion, but Patty convinced me I should keep it myself.

Feeling somewhat less rejected by my birth father's side of the family, I was looking forward to Jeremy's first communion. My parents were going to come up from Long Island and my birth mother was going to fly up, too. We hadn't all been together since my birth mother had been hospitalized two years earlier.

All seemed so right with the world.

CHAPTER TWELVE

In the End Is a Beginning

THE BIRTH OF my fourth child, Kieran, in 1984 had confirmed the miracle and continuity of physical life. For me, as a Catholic, Jeremy's first communion in 1987 confirmed the miracle of the spiritual source of life in the gift of holy communion. On May 16, the day Jeremy was to receive his first communion, another link in the life cycle was forged: my mother died suddenly and unexpectedly at my home.

She and my father had come up on the previous afternoon to attend Jeremy's first communion service, joining my birth mother who had arrived the day before. I was still at work when my parents arrived, and Patty had gone off to work by the time I got home.

My mother remarked casually that when she and my father had pulled into the driveway, she had seen six children playing on the front lawn, when there were actually only three. The double vision disappeared as fast as it came. She dismissed it and chalked it up to riding in the car with the sun in her eyes. She said she didn't really feel well. She was under a doctor's care for a heart condition, but her medication and a visit to the doctor had reassured her that she was doing fine.

Before she went to bed, she said to my father, "If I don't feel better in the morning, I don't think I'll make it to the communion."

He assumed she just wasn't feeling right. I was a little more concerned, but not concerned enough to call for an ambulance.

The next morning, my wife and I were up getting our kids showered and dressed. I came out of the shower and heard my parents' travel alarm buzzing in their room. I waited for the alarm to stop sounding. When it didn't, I looked over at my wife.

"That's funny," I told her.

It was funny, because although my father was hard of hearing, my mother was a very light sleeper. There was no way she would sleep through an alarm. No way that she wouldn't yell over to my father to shut the alarm off.

So I went into their room. My son Nicholas followed me. I went over and turned off the alarm as Nicholas climbed on the bed my father was in. I looked over at my mother. She was asleep on her side, facing the window. I went to her bed and gently shook her foot.

"Nanny," I said, "it's time to get up."

She didn't move or respond in any way.

I shook her foot again.

Still no response.

My initial reaction was to see if she was breathing. I couldn't detect any sign of breathing or pulse. Right then and there I knew she was dead. I quickly left the room and went back into our bedroom where my wife was dressing.

"Patty," I said, trying to remain calm. "I don't want to sound overly dramatic, but I think my mother's dead."

Patty quickly followed me back to my parents'

room to get Nicholas. Since I had left the room, my father had gotten out of bed. He didn't know what had happened. I didn't know how to tell him.

I was standing at my mother's side. My father came over to me, and whether or not he could read my face, he knew something was wrong.

"Nanny's dead," was all I could tell him.

He gave me a panicked look.

"Can't you do anything?" he asked.

I turned my mother onto her back and gave her cardiopulmonary resuscitation, but I knew it was too late. Too late for anything. Death had come quickly and quietly. It had claimed my mother without so much as giving any of us a chance to say "Goodbye."

The cause of death was simple. Her heart had just stopped beating. I thanked God for allowing my mother to have such a peaceful death.

Hundreds of thoughts ran through my head as Patty went to call for an ambulance. I had to subjugate the feelings I had, because there were so many practical things I had to take care of. My father was in a state of shock. I needed to keep an eye on him. At the same time, I had to check on my children, because they knew what had happened before I had a chance to tell them.

It was hardest on Jennifer, not only because she was the oldest, but also because she and my mother were especially close. The boys were aware that something had gone wrong. Nicholas was a little too young to comprehend fully what had happened. Jeremy, who usually internalized everything, was my biggest concern.

This was supposed to have been Jeremy's day—his first communion. A day to celebrate and for him to be the center of attention. Nothing I could do could change what had happened, but I knew my mother would not have wanted Jeremy to miss out on his big day.

Each minute felt like an hour. My mother looked so peaceful, in direct contrast to all the chaos that was going on in the house, especially after the ambulance arrived, followed by the State Troopers.

When all the practical matters had been taken care of, I turned my thoughts to what was going to happen next. I didn't want my father to see my mother carried out of the house. I preferred that the last image he had of her be that of her lying peacefully in bed.

Patty and I decided we would all go to Jeremy's communion service as planned, my father, my birth mother and the children with us. My mother would have wanted it that way.

It turned out to be a good idea, because the priest said the communion mass for my mother. That in itself was a great comfort to my father.

What made the event both tragic and unusual was the fact that my birth mother had also come up for Jeremy's communion. In a way, it was fitting that she should have been there then. Call it coincidence or fate, it was certainly ironic that both mothers should have been in the same house when one of them died. On reflection, I can't help but think how wonderfully odd it was to have my birth mother present at the death of the mother who had raised me.

My mother's death seemed to bring so many things into focus, as a death often does. It makes the trivial all the more trivial, and it makes the things we take for granted so meaningful and fragile.

My mother had never won the New York State

Lottery. She had never played the stock market, had never vacationed at exotic resorts. My mother had cut coupons, she hadn't cut deals. She always felt far more comfortable in a dress off the rack from J. C. Penney's than she ever would have felt in a designer dress by Halston or Perry Ellis.

My mother was never featured in *People Magazine*. She never made the cover of *Time* or *Newsweek*. In the scheme of world politics and international influence, my mother wouldn't have rated a footnote.

My mother was a simple woman. She might not have had the education of an Eleanor Roosevelt or the fame of a Mother Teresa, but that didn't mean she was without influence. When people sought her out—and many people did—it wasn't because she had wise answers to bestow, but because she was so willing to listen with a compassionate ear. She was an anchor in a storm. A good friend. She was a wonderful mother, and a woman who relished her role as "Nanny."

That was my mother. One of the dearest women ever to have graced this often less than perfect world. She taught me more about life than I could ever have learned from books. And although there were times when I wondered if she missed out on life's adventures because she never ventured very far away from home, I realized that you don't really need to be an explorer on the high seas to come to an understanding of the mystery of life.

My mother's death caused me to reflect on my own life's journey. Where had I arrived? How much closer had I come to understanding what life was supposed to be all about? Or was I no closer after all? Did all my searching lead me in the wrong direction?

The death of a loved one, especially that of a parent, challenges you to think about less-than-worldly topics. I was not immune to the hurt of loss.

Even as I write this, six months after my mother's death, I feel an emptiness that can never really be filled. My comfort, however, comes from knowing that death is not the end, but a beginning. Death is the ultimate link that unites us in life temporal and life eternal.

I felt fortunate that my mother and I had never left anything unsaid between us. I didn't have to look forward to a life of regret that I had never let my mother know how I felt about her. Perhaps it was that feeling that led me on to another episode in the search for my missing links.

My mother's death reminded me how fragile life really is, and how easy it is to put matters of importance off to another time. As adamant as my birth mother was in not wanting to make contact with her other child, I could no longer deny myself the right to find that particular missing link. I didn't want to wake up one morning realizing it was too late to do anything about something I could have done years earlier. If I was to find my brother, I was going to have to look for him in the present, not wonder about him in the future.

The few times I had done any "book" searching for my brother, I always looked for him under what would have been his birth father's name. Two months after my mother's death, I began looking for him under my birth mother's name. Sure enough, I found an entry in the record of births for Manhattan that convinced me I had found my brother's birth certificate number.

What convinced me was the fact that under the listing for an Andrew William Hamilton, the code for the birth mother's maiden name was also that of Hamilton. How many women marry a man who shares the same last name? Not enough of them to cause me to think I was about to embark on a wild goose chase.

With my supposed brother's supposed birth certificate number, I called upon someone who happened to know someone who had access to the birth records. I knew enough from experience that any request for an adoptee's birth certificate would result in a copy of an amended birth certificate, not the original birth certificate.

In the case of an adoptee who is looking for his or her original birth certificate to locate birth parents, an amended certificate is a dead end. In my case, however, I didn't need to find my brother's original birth certificate. I knew all about his life before adoption; it was his life after adoption that I was interested in. I hoped to obtain his amended birth certificate, listing his adoptive name along with his adoptive parents' address at the time of his adoption.

Of course, I didn't expect the wheels of progress to move fast. I expected to have to wait a few months before I heard anything. Surprisingly, I got a call after only waiting three days.

"Get a pencil and a piece of paper," my informant told me the afternoon she called me at work. "I have news for you."

I quickly tore a piece of paper from a pad and nearly knocked over my pencil holder as I grabbed for a pencil.

"Your brother's name is Andrew William Larkin. He was adopted by a Mr. and Mrs. J. Benedict Larkin. Mr. Larkin is listed as an attorney."

"Do they list an address?" I asked, knowing full

well that any address listed on my half-brother's birth certificate would more than likely be meaningless forty years later.

"His birth certificate gives 27 Westerly Drive, Warwick, Rhode Island as his address at the time of his adoption."

After I had thanked my informant for all her help, she asked me to tell her how my search for Andrew turned out.

"You'll be one of the first people I'll tell," I said, wondering if I'd ever have anything to tell her.

I wondered that, because I was again in the position of having the power to do something about my search. But it was a power limited by the rights of other people. As I thought about my philosophical dilemma, I realized I was getting ahead of myself. I might have had a name and an address, but that information didn't assure me that I would be able to locate my half-brother easily. There were too many things that could have happened over the years. If somebody had located my birth records with my address at the time of my adoption, they wouldn't have been able to track me down without some keen detective work, because I had moved away from Brooklyn when I was only five years old.

I had serious doubts that Andrew Larkin still resided in Warwick, let alone at 27 Westerly Drive; however, being the optimistic pessimist that I am, I called Warwick Directory Assistance and asked for Andrew's parents, believing that there was more of a chance, albeit a slim one, that they would still be in Warwick. Instead of the operator telling me there was no J. Benedict Larkin living in Warwick, she came back on the line with, "We have a listing for a J. Benedict Larkin on

Rosewood Court in Warwick.''

Willing to tempt fate, I asked her if she might have a listing for an Andrew Larkin.

''The directory shows an Andrew Larkin at 27 Westerly Drive.''

I almost dropped the phone. Not only did Andrew Larkin still live in Warwick, but he also lived at the address listed on his birth certificate.

With two very ''hot'' telephone numbers carefully scribbled on a piece of paper, I began to drum on the side of my desk with my pencil.

''Now what do you do, Sherlock?'' I said to myself. ''You got what you wanted. What's your problem?''

My problem was that I didn't know how to go about making a call to one of those numbers without the risk of hurting somebody. I couldn't assume Andrew knew anything about his adoption. He might not have been told about it. And if that were the case, I would certainly be overstepping the bounds of my own search if I called him up and announced I was his half-brother.

The only logical thing to do was to call his parents and explain the situation and assure them that if Andrew didn't know about his adoption, I would back off from my search.

As I rehearsed my phone call with Andrew's parents, I began to have this overwhelming sense of deja vu. How many times in the last six years had I sat staring at a phone, debating whether to pick up the receiver and wondering what I would say when I did.

When I called Patty and said, ''I did it again,'' she agreed with me that I should call Andrew's parents, when I finally got around to making the call.

I even had to debate whether I was going to ask for Mr. Larkin or Mrs. Larkin. I based my decision on Mr. Larkin's legal profession. As a lawyer, I reasoned, he would understand my position. That's what I hoped when I first dialed the Larkins' number two days after I had obtained it from Directory Assistance. There was no answer that night at eight. Nor at nine, nor again at ten. The same held true when I called the following night and the night after that.

After the sixth attempt to reach the Larkin residence, I had a very morbid thought. What if the Larkins weren't home to answer their phone because they were attending a funeral? I probably would never have thought such a thing if my mother hadn't just died three months earlier, but the thought was very strong in my mind now.

Patty suggested I try to call during the day instead of at night, which was what I did on a Friday afternoon. I dialed the number expecting to get no response. I was wrong. A woman answered. Probably Mrs. Larkin, I thought.

"Good afternoon," I said, trying to sound as cheerful and gentle as possible. "Is Mr. Larkin there, please?"

"He's not here right now," she replied quickly.

"Do you know when he might be home?" I asked.

There was a pause before she said, "Who needs to talk to him?"

I began to feel like a stupid chauvinist. Mrs. Larkin had as much right to be told who I was and why I was calling as did Mr. Larkin. Eventually she would have to find out, and when she did, she might resent the fact that I hadn't told her first when I had the chance.

With a deep breath, I began my spiel.

"This is a difficult phone call to make, Mrs. Larkin, and I hope you'll understand why when I tell you what I have to say. You see, I was adopted when I was an infant, and I learned that I have a half-brother. I have good reason to believe that your son Andrew is my half-brother."

"I think," she said, without hesitating, "you've made a terrible mistake calling us." She was very agitated.

"I'm sorry," I said, not even trying to mask my confusion at her reaction.

"Do you have a lawyer?" she asked.

"Why would I need a lawyer?"

"I suggest you obtain the services of a lawyer and have your lawyer call our lawyer."

"I don't think it's necessary to get a lawyer involved."

"I have nothing more to say."

And even though I made an attempt to mollify her, she wouldn't entertain the thought of pursuing our conversation any further.

My brief phone call with Mrs. Larkin took the wind out of my search for Andrew. I could only imagine that he had never been told about his adoption, or why else would his mother have reacted so vehemently when I told her who I was?

All during my ride home that night, I couldn't help but go over and over the content of my conversation with Mrs. Larkin. Just as my bus was about to pull into my stop, a strange notion occurred to me and made me laugh to myself.

"What if Mrs. Larkin misunderstood me," I thought, "and assumed when I told her I was Andrew's half-brother that I was indirectly implicating Mr. Larkin?"

It was possible. I had no idea about the nature of the Larkins' relationship. Mrs. Larkin could easily have thought I was trying to tell her that I was her husband's illegitimate child.

The first thing Monday morning, I sat down at work and wrote a letter to the Larkins, apologizing for the upset my phone call might have caused them, and assuring them my intentions were honorable. I wrote at length, detailing my story and trying to let them know that I could understand their position if they had never told Andrew about his adoption.

I signed the letter, but didn't give my home address or telephone number, opting rather to leave my business address on the envelope.

Fully expecting never to hear from the Larkins or their lawyer, I was prepared to close off another dead-end in the search for my missing links. I guessed I just wasn't intended to know my half-brother.

I guessed wrong, because three days after I had sent my letter to the Larkins, I got a phone call at home. The caller was Andrew, or Drew as he was known.

The first thought that streaked across my mind like a bolt of lightning was that Drew was calling to tell me off for upsetting his mother. Suddenly I became very apologetic.

"My mother just showed me the letter you sent her," Drew said.

My muscles began to tighten as I prepared to be berated.

"I want to explain my mother's reaction to your

phone call," he began, with compassion, not bile, in his voice. "My mother had just returned home from a week at my sister's house when you called. We had just buried my father."

How small did I feel? If it were possible to crawl under a gnat's belly, I could have done it with a top hat on my head. I couldn't believe my timing. I couldn't believe that my initial hunch about a funeral had been right.

"I'm so sorry," I told him. "If I had known, I wouldn't have called when I did."

"How would you have known? You couldn't have. But you'd have to know my mother to understand her reaction. She was very protective of my father. And when you called, she only imagined the worst. She thought you were some crank who had read his obituary in the paper and was trying to put something over on her."

So she had thought I was saying I was her husband's illegitimate child.

"Your letter did explain everything. And yes, I have always known I was adopted. But I never knew I had a brother."

"How would you have known that? Even if you had had access to your original birth records, it wouldn't have told you anything, because I was born after you."

"How long," Drew asked, "have you known about me?"

"It's been seven years. Ever since I first saw my original birth documents."

"How old were you when you were adopted?"

"I was going on seven months old," I told Drew.

"What about you? I saw on your birth records that you weren't adopted until 1947, but you were born in 1945."

"I was 23 months old when I was adopted."

I wondered what took so long for Drew's adoption.

"Where were you before you were adopted?"

"I was in a foster home on Staten Island."

"Were you adopted from the Foundling?"

"No. I was adopted through Catholic Charities."

"Had you ever thought about looking for your—our—birth mother?"

"I had, but I never did much about it, except for putting my name in one of those adoption registries."

"You had the Hamilton name. Did you know that when you were growing up?"

"Sure I knew it."

"Hadn't you ever thought of tracking down that name?"

"I guess I didn't have the stamina to go through all that, even though I did live in New York City for awhile in the 'Seventies. I probably could have done something then, but I never did."

"Is there anything you'd like to know?" I asked Drew, knowing full well that he must have dozens of questions.

"I grew up knowing two rumors," he explained. "The first was that the Hamiltons were a very rich family; the second that my father was a Catholic priest."

"The first rumor was absolutely untrue. The Hamiltons were far from a wealthy family. With thirteen kids to feed during the Depression, they barely had enough money to exist."

"Does that make the second rumor true?"

"It's something else we have in common. Both of

our birth fathers were priests.''

"My parents always wondered about that. Now we don't have to wonder anymore.''

If there is anything typical of the adoptee, it's the wondering. I'd had my share of wondering, and Drew had had his share. And while most of my wonderings had been put to rest, it was now Drew's turn to find some long-overdue answers to his questions.

Of course Drew had things that he wanted to know about for reasons of his own. He was particularly interested in his ancestors' nationality.

"Were the Hamiltons Irish?'' he asked.

"Our maternal grandmother was Irish and our grandfather was German.''

"Was our grandmother born in Ireland?''

"No, she was born in the United States.''

"Would you know if her mother had been born in Ireland?''

My genealogical research was coming in handy.

"Our grandmother was a third generation American.''

"What about my father's family? Do you know anything about them?''

"I don't know all that much, but I do remember Aunt Joan telling me that his parents were very Irish. They both spoke with a brogue.''

"That's good to hear.''

"Why,'' I finally asked Drew, "do you need to know this?''

"I have a serious interest in Ireland, and I'd like to become a citizen and buy some land there. But the only way I can become an Irish citizen is to prove that either one of my parents or any of my grandparents were born in Ireland.''

''I'll ask Joan if she might be able to get you some proof that your grandparents were actually born in Ireland.''

''That would be great if you could do that.''

''It would be a pleasure.''

And it was a real pleasure talking with Drew. I didn't feel uncomfortable at all with him on the phone. It was like talking to a . . . brother. This brother just happened to be making a trip to New York the following week.

Drew had arranged to be down in New York while his sister and her husband were in the city on business. We agreed to meet on the steps of the New York Public Library on Fifth Avenue.

When Drew arrived in New York that day, he called and told me to meet him by the granite lion that was closest to 41st Street. On any given afternoon during the summer, the steps of the New York Public Library are filled with people. That afternoon was no exception. As I crossed Fifth Avenue and headed toward the lion, I made eye contact with Drew. He started walking toward me. If it was awkward, it was only so for a moment. Once we shook hands and began to walk toward the restaurant I had picked out—an Irish pub— we took up our conversation where we had left off on the phone.

I had brought some pictures of our birth mother along with all the adoption records from St. Clare's. Drew had brought along the adoption file his father had compiled while he was in the process of arranging Drew's adoption.

''My wife told me I have to remember every word

we say so I can tell her all about it when I get back home. I probably should have brought a tape recorder,'' Drew said.

I laughed, because Patty had also instructed me to take some good mental notes so I could fill her in on all the details.

And there were a lot of details. We managed to cover much ground during the hour and a half of our lunch. Everything from physical resemblance—there was some, but not as much as I had hoped for—to our feelings about adoption.

After lunch, Drew and I walked up town to meet his sister at her hotel. We met in the lobby and went across the street to have a drink. Drew's sister Marisa couldn't have been nicer. She reminded me a lot of my own sister. They both were easy to talk to and both had a good sense of humor.

Marisa remarked at how amazed she was that I had been able to find Drew. She was also amazed at the similarities in our backgrounds. But most of all she was pleased that Drew and I had made contact with each other.

We parted friends—and family. We all hoped that we would be able to get together before too much time had passed. Fortunately, I was able to have my family meet Drew's family within the following weeks. Patty and I had scheduled a visit to her brother's family in Massachusetts, not too far from where Drew and his family lived. With some minor adjustments to our plans, we were able to spend the day with Drew's family before moving on to Patty's brother's house.

Drew's wife, Sandy, was a treasure, as was Phil, Marisa's husband. They were two more individuals I was able to add to the roster of warm and genuine people I had met since I first began piecing together my missing links.

After breakfast with Drew, Sandy, and their three children, Patty and I, along with our four children, drove over to the shore where Marisa and Phil lived. And it was there I first met Drew's mother, a charming New Englander. From the moment she opened her mouth, I thought I was in a room with Katharine Hepburn. Both her voice and her mannerisms reminded me of the great actress.

When it was time for us to leave, the only shadow that darkened the day was my birth mother's image. She was the common bond that Drew and I shared, but she was not a part of our day, nor of our new relationship.

Drew understood why there was a problem and that made things a little easier, but it did not answer the question: how and when do I tell my birth mother about Drew?

Even as I write these words, a few months after Drew and I first talked on the phone, I haven't found the way to broach the subject with my birth mother. I want her to know about it, and I want her to be happy about it. I don't want the news to cause her any pain. But by the same token, I don't want to keep the news from her, because I think it's unfair to keep it a secret.

I hope I'll be able to add an epilogue to this book some day. A happy ending to a search that began so innocently seven years ago this month on that dark and stormy night.

At times it doesn't seem possible that seven years have come and gone since that day I first looked over

Mrs. Chin's shoulder at the information on the micro-film reader. At other times, it seems like it all happened in another lifetime to another person.

PART THREE

Before and After

"What did I learn? I learned that
if you go looking for your
heart's desire and you can't
find it in your own back yard,
then you really hadn't lost it
in the first place."

As spoken by Dorothy
to the Good Witch in
The Wizard of Oz

CHAPTER THIRTEEN

A Chosen Baby?

THE SEARCH FOR my missing links proved there was life before my adoption. But is there life after an adoption search? The answer is an unqualified yes. There is definitely life after finding your links.

Usually that's the alpha and omega of an adoptee's story. It's one part seeking and finding the answer to what life was like before adoption and one part incorporating the results of the search into your life. As adoption searches go, the alpha and omega of my story probably form only a variation on the theme of every adoptee's search. In recent years countless other adoptees' stories have appeared in print. Yet, as similar in theme as my story is to those of others, my search is also unique, because it happened to me, not to another adoptee.

My search, which began on the corner of 50th Street and Eighth Avenue at the height of a winter storm in 1980 and stretched across time and space to my half-brother's driveway in Warwick, Rhode Island on a beautiful summer morning in 1987, is only part of my story. It's a narrative with definite dimensions, but lacking in depth if not told in the context of my life as the adoptee I was between the time I was brought home to Madison Avenue in the Flatbush section of Brooklyn to the moment I headed for that fateful intersection on Manhattan's West Side. I wish I could say my life as an adoptee was filled with mystery, adventure, and romance. I wish I could make claims to having done wondrous deeds. I wish I could recall stories that would set your hair on end; stories that would set you laughing; tales that would have you begging for more; parables that would bring a tear to your eye. I only wish that my life could have been as exciting as I always imagined it might have been, if only . . . if only things had happened differently.

Alas, my life would be a lie if I recounted things that only took place in that land bounded by my limitless imagination. I could spin a yarn about things that might have happened, but the cloth fabricated from that yarn would not hold up in the light of truth. And the truth is I am normal, unexceptional, ordinary.

This confession is not meant as an apology, although I sometimes wish I could have accomplished some shining deeds: winning a gold medal for downhill skiing in the Olympics; performing in Oscar-winning films year after year; writing a Pulitzer Prize play; playing first base for the Brooklyn Dodgers; writing a symphony for the New York Philharmonic; discovering an archeological site that would have changed the way the world thought about human history. I wish I could have done something that would really have mattered.

In my Walter Mitty moments, I've stood center stage as the Nobel medal was ceremoniously hung around my neck. In moments of truth, I've stood waiting in the wings. Somewhere between the wishes and the desires is the placid pasture I call my life. The elements from which that life is made can be categorized, examined under a microscope, and pinpointed psychologically. My life, however, has been more than the sum of its parts. My life is a canvas that still has the smell of fresh paint, as well as broad brush strokes and bright colors. The canvas is, as yet, unfinished and untitled. And if the finished piece never hangs in the gallery of renown, it will still be the only portrait of its kind. For that reason alone, my portrait is extremely important.

Anonymity is not a liability. There is no such thing as being a nothing or a nobody, not even in this celebrity-conscious world of fast cars, expensive furs, and high-priced real estate.

From the moment I took my first breath, I had a lifelong commitment to live and love life. The "I" in the "I am" says it all. My life statement has not been limited to saying, "I am an adoptee," because my adoption was not the deciding factor in my life. It played a part, of course, but it was not the star. My adoption was an attribute. It was a mantle I learned to wear; it did not wear me.

I didn't spend my childhood paralyzed by the specter of my adoption. I didn't brood away my youth like some melancholy adolescent. I lived a very typical childhood. I played with toy soldiers. I collected baseball cards. I read Hardy Boys mysteries. I climbed trees and jumped across creeks and streams. I went around collecting empty soda bottles with friends, taking our hard-earned spoils to buy Milky Ways and M&M's. I played baseball in an empty lot around the corner. I strapped on a pair of skates and wobbled around a frozen pond across from the last dairy farm in Seaford.

My childhood is a precious memory, filled with

moments that, to this day, can still warm me with a glow of wonderful innocence. With the passage of time, the recesses of my childhood become more dear to me because I am at the pinnacle of my life. Behind me I can see the young boy I was. The little boy with the crew-cut and the big old red two-wheeler. Ahead of me I can see my certain destiny, and while there are times when I am filled with the fear of growing old, there is a voice inside me that says, "Fear not. You are not going to a place where life ends, but where life begins anew."

There have been moments when I've been touched by something I can't even explain. Mystics might have a name for it. Men of great faith might be able to explain it. But for me, those special moments are just glimpses of immortality.

I've always looked forward to those moments and tried to be receptive to them. If I had to point to anything that seemed to me to make me different, it would be that I could never take a single moment in life for granted. There was, and still is, something so precious about life that I am not able to consider any of it inconsequential. Admittedly, it is my weakness, and it is also my strength. Whether I wanted to or not, I've always listened with my heart. I've always been vulnerable. I wear my heart on my sleeve.

There have been times when I wondered whether my "sensitive nature" was directly related to my adoption. I would wonder if the person I had become was the direct result of my adoption. Or had I become that person because of the way I perceived my adoption? If I had grown up not knowing I had been adopted, would I have become the person I am?

The answer to that question would be purely speculative, because I grew up knowing I had been adopted. Trying to imagine who I might have been if I hadn't been adopted is a doubtful activity at best.

Did the knowledge of my adoption have a dramatic effect on my personality development? Not that I know of. The fact of my adoption was not a bombshell dropped on me when I was a teenager. Knowledge of my adoption has always been part of my consciousness. I never remember not knowing I had been adopted. And how did I first find out I was adopted? I don't remember. I didn't know then that I might ever have reason to have perfect recall of the event. I didn't take notes.

My father was not dressed in a forest-green smoking jacket when he called me into his oak-paneled den to discuss my adoption. He had neither a forest-green smoking jacket, nor an oak-paneled den. My parents and I never had a heart-to-heart talk about adoption. My mother never looked up from the kitchen counter where she was mixing cookie dough to tell me, "By the way, Vincent, you were adopted."

My first memories about adoption came from *The Chosen Baby*, the innovative and definitive adoption story by Valentina P. Wasson. Whatever attitudes, perceptions, misconceptions, and prejudices I had as a youngster about adoption could be found between the covers of *The Chosen Baby*.

I don't actually remember my parents reading the book to me, but I do have clear and distinct memories about reading the book myself. And I didn't read it just once. I read it over and over again, until the message was deeply embedded in my consciousness.

Again, I can't remember the specific moment

when the light went on in my little blond head that the story was about me, but I do vaguely remember reading the book more as a lesson than as a story.

The problem with memories is the nature of memory itself. I have some very specific memories that have been recorded verbatim in this book. Memories that play themselves out without ever a single change. Then there is my "memory bank," my recollections not of singular events, but of repetitive occasions. Christmases, birthdays, and summer vacations are stored in this memory bank. Each of these memories is an anthology. When I think of Christmas, I don't think about any one Christmas in particular; I remember all the Christmases of my childhood rolled into one.

When I close my eyes, I can see myself as a five-year-old in Brooklyn, hugging a big brown teddy bear. Immediately I turn into a ten-year-old trying on a new pair of skates. Then I'm a teenager studying the instructions for a microscope. Back and forth. From glimpses of Christmases long gone to the last Christmas my mother spent with my family and me, I have an ever-growing Christmas memory.

I can turn a dial in my "memory bank" to a generic point called "childhood," and I see myself at various ages during various stages of my growth. When I think of my childhood, I think of a corner candy store that was near my home. I can't calculate the number of miles my friends and I put on our bicycles making pilgrimages to that little store, but if frequent-flyer programs had been in place back then for bicyclists, we'd have earned a free trip to Europe each. As many trips as I took to that candy store, there isn't any one particular trip I can remember. All I have is an image of me on my bike. I'm wearing a striped polo shirt and khaki pants. I have two old baseball cards clipped to the front and back of my bicycle with clothespins, because the sound of the cardboard against the spokes of the wheel makes the bike sound like a motorcycle.

When I try to focus in on my face, I never see the same face for very long, because the image changes age before I can isolate it for a closer examination.

The Chosen Baby is part of my "memory bank" in one way, but it's also part of my specific memories. I can't remember any particular moments in my childhood when the book was read to me or, after I learned how to read, when I read it to myself. *The Chosen Baby*, however, is specific, because I can remember, with a certain degree of accuracy, the book itself and what it had to say.

And what it had to say went way beyond the actual story of a childless couple adopting a child from an adoption agency. That part was clear, simple, and direct. The story couldn't have been any nicer or sweeter. And if the purpose of the book was to establish the concept of adoption as something very positive, *The Chosen Baby* accomplished that task. The book, however, failed to establish adoption in the context of reality.

It must be remembered that the book, originally published in 1939, was as much a product of its time as it was a force in its time. It should be further pointed out that Wasson rewrote *The Chosen Baby* in 1950 when the Trumans were in the White House, when television was entering its golden age, and when normalcy abounded in all walks of life. Under those circumstances, even though it was considered innovative, *The Chosen Baby* was about as controversial as a bowl of cream-o'-wheat.

Editorial copy on the dust jacket of the book stated, ". . . this little story about adoption, written *for* (the editor's italics) children has brought joy and understanding to adopted children everywhere, and for foster parents has been of immeasurable help in solving the *problem* (my italics) of how to best begin to tell a child that he was 'chosen' (the editor's quotation marks)."

What's probably most interesting in that jacket copy is the editor's belief that telling a child that he was "chosen" (chosen, mind you, not adopted) was a problem. I can only wonder why telling a child he was chosen/adopted was a "problem." And if it was a problem, who created the problem?

I can speculate. I can also indicate other areas in the story that pose some problems for me. As early as the third sentence of the book, the author, in describing the fictional Mr. and Mrs. Brown, wrote:

> They had been married for many years. They had been as happy as could be and were still young, and only one thing was wrong. They had no babies of their own, although they always longed for a baby to share their home.

". . . Only one thing was wrong. They had no babies of their own. . . ." Now if that isn't a telling comment on the childless state, I don't know what is.

Further along in the story, the plot thickens. After waiting an unspecified amount of time, the Browns get a phone call from the adoption agency. They go to the agency. The woman at the agency tells the Browns:

> "Now go into the next room and see the baby. If you find that he is not *just the right baby for you*

(author's italics), tell me so and we shall try and find another."

The Browns go into the other room and immediately fall in love with the baby.

Mrs. Brown picked him up and sat him on her lap and said, "This is our Chosen Baby. We don't need to look any further."

Some selective choosing is all I can say. And ditto when it came time for the Browns to "choose" a sister for their adopted son.

Although not in a league with *Ben Hur*, *Wuthering Heights*, and *Gone With the Wind*, *The Chosen Baby* did make an impression on me. But the problem with a lasting impression is that the impression remains as it was in your childhood, while you continue to grow and begin to think like an adult.

For that reason I would have to say *The Chosen Baby* was a very good book for children who had been adopted, but not such a good book for the adults those children grew into years later. In painting a picture-perfect view of adoption, it didn't allow any room for the facts of adoption. Nowhere in the book was there any mention of birth parents. It was as if they didn't exist. The role of the adopted child was a passive role. The adoptive parents, although never called that in the book, were also passive. The only active character in the book was the social worker. Almost godlike in her powers, the social worker played the key role in *The Chosen Baby*. She had the ultimate decisions in her hands. She could either give thumbs up or thumbs down to the "adoptive parents-in-waiting."

As a child, I was not able to analyze the book as I

did when I grew older. Because the book never gave a second thought to the birth parents, I never gave them even a first thought. They were never a part of my childhood consciousness. In the adoptee's "facts of life," life began after adoption. That's what the book implied, and that's what formed my initial adoptive conceptions. When I stopped thinking like a child, the gossamer wings that had once elevated the ethereal suppositions in *The Chosen Baby* to a level of infallibility buckled under the weight of logic.

The book would have led the reader to believe that all adoptions were ordained in heaven. It would have convinced you that childless couples adopted a poor or-phaned baby without any ulterior motives. Their act of kindness, in taking in an "unwanted child," was the epitome of charity. I wouldn't want to say there was no charity involved, but I would have to say that charity was not the prime mover in the adoption story. A child-less couple adopted a child because they couldn't have a child of their own. That statement is not meant to be a cruel commentary. It's a fact of life. The rare couples who actually did adopt because they wanted to give a homeless child a home of his or her own and parents to call "mom" and "dad" were very, very few and far, far between. I'd even go so far as to say that the majority, a big majority, of childless couples who went on to adopt wouldn't ever have entertained the notion of adoption if they'd had a child of their own.

A childless couple in the 1940's and 1950's wanted to adopt because for some reason or another, they weren't able to have a child of their own. Back then marriage and child-bearing were not separate entities. One naturally came with the other. A woman who arrived at a marriageable age in the 1940's and 1950's usually had been raised to believe that her destiny was to become a wife and mother. There was no room in her life for a career. And if she chose a career, she rarely married. Very few couples back then, especially if they were raised as Catholics, ever made a conscious decision that their marital union would exclude children. If a married couple were confronted with the fact that they could not have a child of their own, the thought of a childless marriage was, in most cases, not acceptable. Both the man and woman believed that their lives were incomplete until baby made three.

Adoption, then, was not really intended to serve the child, but rather the childless couple. To foster the myth that it was otherwise would be to make a delicate fabrication.

My parents were not unlike other married couples of their day. My mother had always dreamed of having children. She even held a secret wish to have twins. The same mind-set held true for my father. He married thinking that a child would automatically come with the job. Their decision to adopt was based on a missing element in their marriage. In essence they concluded, "If we can't have a child of our own, we'll adopt." They didn't arrive at that conclusion by saying, "Why don't we make a home for a parentless child?" although that's what they ultimately did—for two children. And however debatable the semantics might be, the fact remains that adoption was a couple's solution to infertility—not being able to have a child—but not a solution to the child's homeless family-less state.

With that said, I should add that the reason behind my parents' decision to adopt did not make them lesser parents; indeed it reflected their humanity. Their desire and need to have a child were normal. They never considered adoption as an alternative to having a child of their own; they considered it one of two ways to have a child. It was never a matter of choosing; it was a matter of settling.

My parents, along with countless couples who found themselves in a similar predicament, never deliberately chose adoption as a way of creating their families. Adopting parents also never, except in rarest instances, chose the babies they adopted.

You can go to the local supermarket and choose the cantaloupe you want, or you can go to a Chevy dealer and choose the make and model car you might want to buy, but back in the era when my parents were trying to adopt, there was no choosing of babies. My parents were told there was a baby available to them for adoption. The child in question was a two-week-old girl, born Patricia Janice Dowden. My parents took two-week-old Patricia home with them. Two years later they got another call that their name had reached the top of the list and another baby was waiting to be picked up at the Foundling. In the case of the second call, seven-month-old Edward Donahue went home as Vincent Begley, junior.

Where was the great choosing? Had my parents shopped around, going from one adoption agency to another looking for the "perfect" baby? No, they hadn't. They took both my sister and me home from the Foundling without ever having seen us before the day they picked us up. So what was all this hype about "chosen babies?" Was it a deliberate lie? Or was it a more digestible bromide in a socially touchy situation that involved illegitimacy, unwed mothers, and dastardly fathers?

It was, in my opinion, the sugar coating around the bitter adoption pill. It was supposed to make the adopted child feel better, to compensate for the fact that the child was initially "unwanted."

Unfortunately, that was neither the case nor the truth. In trying to compensate for a sociological situation that went against the grain of convention (unwed motherhood), the adoptee was fed a line of unadulterated blarney. It was no accident that the character of the birth mother never appeared in *The Chosen Baby*, nor was she ever mentioned. Since the book was all about being chosen, there was no room in the story for the concept of giving up a baby. The only choosing in the adoption story, both real and in the book, was done by the people who decided which couples adopted which babies. This choosing was semi-scientific at best, and developed along the lines of a biased philosophy.

The adoption philosophy of the day was not wrong in itself. Although the philosophical intentions might seem noble in theory, in long-term practice they were exclusive and excluding. Rather than draw attention to the fact that a couple had adopted a child, most adoption agencies went out of their way to provide the couple with a child who could have been their own child by birth. Everything possible was done to pick up where nature left off. If a dark-haired, olive-skinned couple had been accepted as adoptive parents, the child "chosen" for them would have had similar coloring. Rarely, if at all, would a blond-haired, blue-eyed baby with a creamy white complexion have been the "choice" for them.

My sister and I look enough alike to be biological siblings. We might not have had our parents' physical characteristics, but we could easily have been "mistaken" for their biological children.

Was there anything wrong with this process? Was it immoral or illegal? No, there was nothing immoral or illegal about it, but it did smack of prejudice, including prejudice against adoption. It was so much easier to let the world think the child was yours than have to explain, as if there were a real need to explain—or apologize—for having an adopted child.

My parents were never embarrassed about having adopted my sister and me, but the social customs of the day made it difficult for them to feel comfortable about having adopted.

How comfortable did I feel about being adopted? In the beginning, I felt neither comfortable nor uncomfortable. I simply felt loved, the way a child is loved by his parents. I felt the same way I hope my children feel. I hope they feel loved and wanted, because that's the way children should feel. There is no such thing as "natural" parental love, however, though the love shown children by their parents should be all of a piece, knowing no differences and no boundaries. It is not selective, and it does not, if it is a true parental love, "choose."

My parents loved my sister and me unconditionally. There was never a feeling that they loved us more or less because we were adopted. They never made us feel different. And they never made us feel special. Whatever differences I might have had with my parents were the same differences any child has with his or her parents.

So, if I was such a normal child, why, as an adult, did I feel so adamant against the "chosen baby" syndrome? The answer isn't easy, because it's hard to pin down an unconscious feeling. I began to resent the idea of being a "chosen" baby when I learned what the opposite of the word "chosen" might be. I began to resent the concept when I learned that "chosen" was a wolf in sheep's clothing.

Because I bought the notion that I was a "chosen" baby, I also had to buy the idea that I could become an "unchosen" baby. If my parents had chosen me as their child, couldn't they just as easily decide to "unchoose" me . . . send me back from whence I came?

My parents never would have done that, and unlike some of the adoptive parents I have read about, they never threatened me with my adoption. They never used it against me as a weapon to control my behavior.

That doesn't mean, however, there weren't times when I didn't worry about being "unchosen." Subconsciously, I knew my parents were all-knowing and all-powerful. I knew there was a difference between being born to your parents and being adopted by them. Whenever a relative or family friend would off-handedly remark how grateful I should feel because I was adopted, I translated "grateful" into "obligated." I felt I had to do more than "normal" kids to show my appreciation for having loving parents, even though my parents never made me feel obligated to them at all. Still, there were times when I couldn't help but feel obligated. Hadn't they "chosen" me out of all the available babies in the world? Wasn't I special? Wasn't I so special and blessed that I had to do everything within my childlike powers to deserve the chosen title?

It was an obligated feeling I sometimes wished I could wash away. There is no reason why any child should have to feel obligated to his or her parents for the gift of life. Nor just because an adoptee's gift came by another route, is there any reason why he or she should feel obligated to the adoptive parents.

My children are my children. They have no basic obligation to me just because they were born to my wife and me. They had nothing to do with that. They didn't ask to be born. We wanted them, but in wanting them, we had to want them without any strings attached. That doesn't mean my children don't have responsibilities. They do. They have growing responsibilities, and part of those include a responsibility to me. But they don't owe me anything. They might think, erroneously, I believe, that they have to thank me one day for providing them with food, clothing, and shelter, but they'll never have to thank me for giving them life. There are no parental pre- and post-payments. It's not a job nor a task. My children never have to worry about being "unchosen." There is no "back" where I can send them, although there are times when I don't know what to do with them and wish there were a place I could send them for an hour or two. But that's all part of being a parent, and the same holds true for being a child.

I know there are times when my children wish they could send me away for an hour or two. I know there are times when my parental powers get under their skins. And I know there are times when they get angry with me. And, yes, there have been times when they've told me they don't like me, and a few times they've even blurted out that they "hate" me. In those

172

blurting moments, I can sense the guilt they feel, because no child wants to hate a parent. There are enough built-in obligations in a parent-child relationship without our magnifying them by putting them into words.

The difference between my children and the child I was can be found in the safety net my wife and I have provided them. It's the safety net that comes to a couple's birth children. No matter the differences, no matter the ups and downs, our children know they belong "with" my wife and me.

As an adoptee, I didn't always feel the presence of that safety net. There were times when I felt I had to go that extra mile, do that extra chore, be that extra special child to earn and keep my place. I may have been wrong to think that way, but tell me that thirty years ago when I was living it. Don't tell me that today after the damage has been done.

Damage? There was damage done? Yes, and unfortunately, it was self-inflicted and unnecessary. Unnecessary because, if I had known better, I would have known that I had as much of a safety net as any other kid. Self-inflicted, because I allowed myself to become a slave to my obligations.

I might have been adopted, and I might even have been adopted by an ideal couple, but that didn't seem to compensate for the obligations I felt. It was even small comfort to learn later that I wasn't alone in those feelings. Other adoptees had them. My own sister had them, but she, too, never voiced her feelings, because as an adoptee she also felt obligated to silence.

What made this over-zealous service to obligations so harmful was the fact that it became part of my personality code. I also always seemed to have to become obligated in all my extra-familial relationships. I always made a conscious effort to be accepted. I sometimes think I unconsciously wanted to be chosen all over again each time I formed a new relationship or became part of a new group.

No matter how secure I should have felt, I often managed to feel temporary. Whether it was a matter of not feeling deserving or just a tendency to insecurity, I can't say.

My feelings may have been part of my basic personality and nothing to do with my being adopted. I can't say, because I don't know how I might have turned out under different circumstances. All I do know is that I frequently suffered from a slight orphan complex. I sometimes seemed to think the reason for my existence was to please others; in pleasing others, I was supposed to find satisfaction.

I later came to realize that the desire to please and be pleasing and the need to satisfy other people's expectations was as much tied to my religious code as it was to my adoptee code. I felt, whether wrongly or rightly, that as a Catholic, I was supposed to relish my lot in life, whether good or bad, and let "God's will be done." It took me a long time to realize that I had a stock in my own future. It took some painful growth to come to the realization that my destiny was not a matter for a committee; it was a personal matter that could be controlled and directed by me.

Instead of learning all this when I was younger and when I really needed it to weather the storms that toss us during adolescence, I learned it later in life, when learning means conscious changing, and such changing becomes a challenge.

All these feelings and self-debates were not part of my conscious childhood. I didn't brood over these matters. I never stopped and wondered whether this feeling or that feeling was the result of my reaction to my adoption or if it was part of the normal cycle of life. I was an actor in the play, I wasn't an objective critic. I had a hard enough time as it was growing up, without having the additional burden of understanding it all.

If I could go back and change only one aspect of my youth, however, I wouldn't change the fact that I was adopted. I would only change my sense of obligations. I sometimes wish I could go back to my grade school days when one of my teachers was reprimanding a fellow student.

"Richard Cox, if you don't get back in your seat now, I'm going to have you write, 'I will not walk around in class' one hundred times tonight as a punishment." She would continue, "I just wish you could be good like Vincent."

Suddenly, as I heard my name brought into the reprimand, I would come crashing back to earth, shot out of my beautiful daydreams. I would blush a crimson red as my name was spoken. Thirty little faces would turn away from the teacher and stare at me.

This sudden notoriety frightened me to the very soles of my Buster Brown shoes. Richard Cox was no longer the central character in the teacher's daily class struggle. I was now standing center stage, not knowing what my next line or action should be.

"Yes," the teacher would go on, "Vincent's a good boy. Richard should be more like Vincent, shouldn't he, class?"

Thirty little heads would nod in unanimous agreement. When the teacher wasn't looking, the thirty little heads would sympathetically look over at Richard, commiserating with him. Richard would look over at me, his eyes open wide, hatred written all over his face. And I would sit there dumbfounded, because I didn't know what I had done to be singled out as a model of "goodness."

Sure, I sat in my seat, never getting up unless I was told to do so. I never talked back or out of turn. I was polite, obedient, and in every way a teacher's ideal student. Not really, though. I was petrified of doing anything wrong for fear of being banished to the far corners of hell, or worse, getting sent to the principal's office. (God, if that had ever happened to me, I probably would have died there on the spot. To be reprimanded in public would have been death by embarrassment.)

The alternative was not nirvana, either. To be publicly declared "good" was to invite the wrath of many fellow students. And if the public declaration wasn't bad enough, the confusion about the label "good" was worse yet. I never knew what I did to be called "good." Surely, I used to think, goodness had to be more than being a bump on a log. Goodness had to be more than doing nothing.

Unfortunately, because goodness-equals-doing-nothing was the message I was sent, that was the message I took as gospel. To be good meant to be inactive. To be bad meant to be like Richard Cox who would get up from his chair and talk out loud. Goodness was passive—that's what I grew up thinking, and that's what I "adopted" as part of my code of behavior. I assimilated that message and went on to think that if I were "good," i.e., if I didn't rock the boat, I would benefit from my "goodness"—that it would be repaid in kind.

Wrong. Good things don't come your way because you're good. And goodness is not passive. Goodness is the result of positive and deliberate actions. Just because I might have avoided "bad" behavior did not automatically make me good—it just made me "not bad."

As a professional "good" boy, I wondered where my future lay and how I would best fulfill my potential. The answer was to be found in a vocation. A calling to the religious life seemed to be a logical course for me to take, considering the path I was on as a child. My vocation was not something I dreamt up alone. Many friends and relatives thought I had the makings of a priest, because I was so *good*.

I was the good little adopted boy who ate all his spinach and never went to bed without brushing his teeth and saying his prayers. I was the good little adopted boy who took this vocation thing seriously. I was the good little adopted boy whose dresser top looked like the back lot of a Hollywood set for a religious epic, because it was cluttered with the religious statues I collected.

That was me in the making. That was the good little adopted boy who was getting his start in life on the wrong foot.

CHAPTER FOURTEEN

*Portrait of the Adoptee
as a Young Man*

AT A TENDER age I was convinced, or at least I had convinced myself, that I had the Midas touch. Everything I touched seemed to turn into a muffler. Call it the after-effects of negative thinking, but I had become my own worst enemy. Where there were no problems, I sometimes envisioned them. Where there were no fire-breathing dragons to be slain, I was out looking for them.

From my vantage point—the only vantage point I had—I imagined the world to be the way I perceived it. As a child, I was a hapless victim set adrift on a rolling sea.

I spent very little time brooding about my adoption. In fact, I can hardly remember times during my preteens when I thought about it at all. I had bigger things to worry about. Pages of long division to work, Citizenship Education tests to study for, people to meet, and places that ten- and eleven-year-olds visit.

Adoption was a silent factor in my life, rearing its tired head only on rare occasions, and on those rare occasions, the specter of adoption was not ominous; it was merely a curiosity. I didn't make a big thing about my adoption. My peers never tormented me with it, because most of them never knew I had been adopted, and when word finally leaked out, it was rather anti-climactic. I do, however, remember the day the news got around. We were playing touch football in front of my house when Bobby asked me if I was adopted. As surprised as I was to hear him ask the question, I was amazingly cool about it.

"Yes," I told Bobby, "I'm adopted."

"Oh," was all he said as we continued to play the game.

That was that. There was no further discussion. No intent to isolate me because I was "different." The earth didn't open up and swallow me whole. My unintentionally kept secret was out in the open.

I went to bed that night basically the same person I had been the night before, only slightly altered, because I was different. Different by virtue of the fact that, other than my sister, I knew no adoptees.

Years later, I learned that a couple down the street had two adopted children, both much younger than my sister and I, and another couple down at the other end of the street also had an adopted daughter. She, too, was much younger.

The fact that there were other adoptees in my immediate world might have made a difference if I had known and if the other adoptees had been closer to my age. Even if the conditions had been altered to fit my case, though, I don't think I would have formed an adoptees' club, because I was still too young to know the questions I would have when I was a teenager.

When I was old enough to have formulated some questions about adoption, there were no fellow adoptees to be found. Or, if there were, they didn't make their presence known to me.

Of the 800 people I went to high school with, I never met a single adoptee. I'm sure there must have been other adoptees in my high school, but since none of us had distinguishing features, or wore special "adoptee outfits," we were unidentifiable in that homogeneous group of teenagers.

The best thing that happened to me as a teenager was my decision to attend a parochial high school. I didn't feel comfortable in the public junior high school I had attended, and the prospect of spending four years in the local public senior high school sent a chill up and down my spine every time I thought about it.

Getting into the Catholic high school of my choice was not an easy matter. A poor test-taker to begin with, I was up against students from Catholic grade schools who had been drilled in how to take the high school entrance exam. From the four high schools I had applied to, I received four rejections. I took those rejections personally; adoptees tend to have difficulty handling any type of rejection.

Because I was still determined to make the big change, some strings were pulled and some concessions were made to get me into St. Agnes Cathedral High School, Class of 1966. Although I was ranked at the bottom of the class, I didn't care. I had made it. I quickly learned that making it and making it happen are miles apart.

Like a burdened salmon I swam the journey upstream against the mighty current. For the first time in my life, I didn't view obstacles or adversities as obstructions to happiness and fulfillment. It would take a certain measure of strength in the struggle to make my way from the bottom of the class into the upper ranks.

My change in attitude was reflected in my change of perception about adoption. As a teenager, afflicted with the doubts that plague all teenagers, I relished the challenge of doing something with my life. For the first time, I began to look at adoption as something more than a singular event in my life. I had always thought it was something that had been done to me once and was completed once my parents had filled out the adoption papers. I was an adoptee, and that did make me different. Not better. Not worse. But definitely different.

In high school, the notion of being a "chosen baby" was killed off forever. I was no longer an adopted child; I was an adopted teenager on the way to becoming an adopted adult. Unfortunately, the vernacular of the time didn't include words for adopted teenager or adopted adult. The mind-set of the day forever locked the concept of adoption into a preschool vocabulary. Because no common language existed for and about growing adoptees, and because the adoption issue was never thought to be a real issue, there wasn't much I could do about being adopted. Besides, I was not obsessed with my adoption. It never amounted to much in my mind, though I would think about it now and again. And my thinking was usually limited to romantic fantasies.

While I might not have thought directly about the adoption experience, I was busy enduring the rites of passage from childhood into the adult world. In assessing my place in the future, in trying to determine what I was all about, I sometimes did find myself wondering what life itself was all about. I assumed that my fellow classmates were having similar thoughts. Though we never really openly addressed the issues of growing up,

I felt a bond with my friends and classmates, at the same time that I felt isolated.

My interest in the priesthood had dissipated by my junior year in high school, leaving me to wonder what I was going to do with the rest of my life. I had hoped for some kind of sign, some divine inspiration that would set me on the right path toward eternal happiness. Such a sign never occurred, although I did find direction in the world of literature. My obsession, if I had one as a teenager, was reading. I devoured and digested every book I could get my hands on. I began to see that there was a miraculous power in the written word. Writers became my source of inspiration. They put my own thoughts into words.

My search first began in the pages of books. I journeyed with the great authors as they sought to unravel life's many mysteries. The more I read, the more I wondered; the more I wondered, the more I needed and wanted to read. I was convinced that I could find the answer to life's complex questions in the pages of books. Not just any books, but books by authors who were compelled to embark on searches to put meaning into their lives.

By the time I had graduated from St. Agnes, I was not the same person who had entered the school as an insecure freshman. Nor was my metaphysical transformation complete when I received my diploma. I still knew I had miles to go before I would ever—if I ever would—discover the source or meaning of my life. And while my quest might have seemed remote and impractical, my desire to become a seeker was already playing a very important part in my life.

The thought of an adoption search was not part of

the package. When I entered Marist College in the fall of 1966, I was not nearly prepared to search for my missing links. I was still too involved with my own personal search to contemplate an adoption search, although I was becoming more aware of how my adoption experience—or how my perception of the adoption experience—had affected me.

And if there was any one aspect of my personality that I wanted to change, it was an aspect that I believed was a result of my adoption perception.

I went off to Marist College alone. No one else from my high school went there. I didn't know a single person at the college when I arrived.

Instead of being overwhelmed by the aloneness of the experience, I took it as my first real baptism of fire. I had to make a name for myself. I had to clear the underbrush and make my own path. The only pathfinders I had to rely upon were the men and women who wrote the words in the new books I discovered in college. By the end of my sophomore year, I felt I had arrived at a new level in my search. I had gained more confidence, but there was something missing, something I could feel but couldn't put into words. What I needed, but didn't know at the time, was a greater challenge than the one being offered me on campus. I needed something that would stretch my capabilities and uncap my potential.

I found that challenge in an opportunity to spend my junior year studying abroad. I was offered the chance to start a new program for Marist at Oxford University. The thought of spending a year at such a renowned university excited and frightened me at the same time. The only thing that kept me from jumping at the chance without any hesitation was the opportunity I knew I had if I stayed on campus for my third year. If I returned to Marist during my junior year, I would be hired as a student admissions counselor. I would be one of the editors of the newspaper and yearbook, and I would be appointed to a position in the student government.

All those things were known quantities. A year at Oxford represented a total unknown. My decision to opt for the unknown came to me when I tried to project my life a few years into the future. If I didn't take the chance to go to Oxford, I knew I would always regret not having seized the opportunity. Whatever opportunities awaited me at Marist would still be there in one form or another when I returned for my senior year.

The first memory I have of my year abroad is as clear today as it was that September morning in 1968 when I stood on the deck of MS *Aurelia* as it pulled out of New York harbor past the Statue of Liberty.

There was no turning back. My world was slowly disappearing as the ship moved out to the open seas. Ahead of me was an uncharted sea. I was embarking on an adventure, a search of my own. The pages that I would turn over would be the pages in my life, not the pages of a book.

I can remember feeling so alone that afternoon as I stood looking out at the endless sea. The only real friend I had with me was a book I had carried up on the deck. It was a volume of Edgar Lee Masters' *Spoon River Anthology*, a collection of poems which told first-person stories of the inhabitants of a small midwestern cemetery. Some of the poems were sad, some were funny, and some were tragic.

For no conscious reason, I opened the book to a poem entitled "George Grey."

> I have studied many times
> The marble which was chisled for me—
> A boat with a furled sail at rest in a harbor.
> In truth it pictures not my destination
> But my life.
> For love was offered me and I shrank
>   from its disillusionment;
> Sorrow knocked at my door, but I was afraid;
> Ambition called me, but I dreaded the chances.
>
> Yet all the while I hungered for meaning in my life.
> And now I know that we must lift the sail
> And catch the winds of destiny
> Wherever they drive the boat.
> To put meaning in one's life may end in madness,
> But life without meaning is the torture
>   of restlessness and vague desire . . .
> It is a boat longing for the sea and yet afraid.

I was not a great believer in fate, but you would have had a hard time convincing me that I wasn't meant to read that poem at that particular time. Not only did the imagery accurately describe my situation, but also the poet's meaning was the essence of my life at the time. I was George Grey. I did hunger for meaning in my life. I did shrink from love's disillusionments. I was afraid of opportunity's knock on my door, and I did dread the chances of ambition's call.

Never before in my life had I lifted my sails to catch the winds of destiny. My boat had been safely tied up in a secure harbor—a boat with a furled sail at rest in a harbor.

That was an accurate assessment of my life and my

destination. Unless I was willing to risk "madness," unless I was willing to toss caution to the winds and seek the limits of my potential, I was never going to be anything more than a man with an unrequited dream.

Edgar Lee Masters' "George Grey" became the foundation for my year at Oxford. It became a reason to search, not an excuse to become irresponsible. Just because I was willing to lift my sails did not mean that I was going to abandon my moral and ethical foundations.

I was more than willing to experience life to the fullest. I was not, however, willing to experiment with the drug counterculture that was absorbing so many other young people in 1968. Nor was I going to grow my hair down to my waist and join some group that espoused free love.

During the great sexual revolution that took the late 1960's by storm, I was a conscientious objector, by choice. I wanted to keep my search pure and metaphysical. I had no intention of seeking and destroying. Even though I believed, and still do believe, that there is room to review those things we hold to be sacrosanct, change—just for the sake of change—is not the answer. I was more interested in seeking and discovering the good that was in the world and the good that might be in me.

As happens in any venture toward discovery, the road to awareness was not without its potholes. After only a few days in Oxford, a few days alone with nobody but me, myself, and I, I learned that the me didn't know myself, and the I was a total stranger.

Before arriving in England I had lived a life of relative simplicity. I had defined myself in terms of things common to my personal experience. I was a young American male. A Catholic. A college student. A son. A brother. An adoptee. I was always something in relation to something else. While I was still all those things in England, the geographical distance made a difference in my points of reference. Stripped of the security of those definitions, I was forced to face the cold, hard fact that I was a nothing. When I was hit by the full impact of my personal discovery, I was left weak at the knees, but not defeated. In fact, I was inspired, because there was no place for me to go but up.

Each day was a new day with a new beginning. Everything seemed to take on a new look. I read things with deeper insights. I met people with an open mind. And I traveled around Europe soaking up everything around me.

My year abroad was my personal renaissance. I returned a different—and yes, I think a better—person, because I returned dedicated to the proposition that all human beings are seekers, and that all men and women are obligated to help each other seek. Nothing, I thought, was ever going to diminish my zest for life. I was prepared to tilt with windmills. I was ready to convert the world.

Little did I know how thin an armor idealism makes when one is Don Quixote battling the forces of cynicism and complacency. Little did I know that my new-found philosophy of life would be challenged so quickly after my victorious return from Europe. Not that I never expected to be challenged, but I didn't expect the first shot to be fired by someone I thought was on my side—a neighbor and friend of my parents.

I had always thought she liked me. Maybe she did.

Maybe she thought she was doing me a favor by being open and honest with me. We were sitting on her front stoop talking about my year abroad when the conversation turned to what I planned on doing with my life after I graduated from college.

"I'd like to be a writer," I told her.

She looked over at me, flashing a restrained smile that said, "You've got to be kidding."

"A writer?"

"I'd like to write for a newspaper, but eventually I'd like to write a book or a play."

The restrained smile grew into a broad grin.

"Forgive me for saying this, but what could you ever write about?"

Like a blast from a large calibre gun, the shot caught me by surprise.

"What the hell," I thought to myself, "does she mean by that? I could write about a lot of things."

"You could never be a writer," she continued, "because you have nothing to say."

Her second volley ripped into me, all but deflating my buoyant spirits of a few seconds before.

Then came the heavy artillery.

"Okay, maybe you were adopted, but that's about all you might ever be able to write about."

I don't remember much of the conversation after that. I think I remained talking with her the amount of time a polite person customarily talks after they've been (unconsciously?) insulted. Then I took a look at my watch and made some remark about having to go home and walk the family aardvark, or some other equally ridiculous remark.

What I remembered then, I still remember today.

A person might change. A person might grow and develop, but the signs of development are often invisible to the eyes of others, even those who supposedly know us best. In this woman's eyes I was still this amorphous little kid. Since she had never seen any evidence of my potential, she had no reason to believe in me or in what I could accomplish. I could understand that. I could even forgive her for her insensitive transgression against my changed self. I was even willing to make allowance for her uneducated remark about my not having anything to say as a writer.

It wasn't her fault that she was under the misguided illusion that in order to be a writer you had to be a misfit or an outcast. She was raised to believe that writers were not normal, you-and-I kinds of people. Writers lived in drafty lofts in Greenwich Village. Writers suffered for their art. Writers lived on the edge of insanity.

I lived in a split-level house in the middle of suburbia. And I don't think I was insane. But, in this woman's estimation, I didn't have any of the makings of a writer . . . with one exception. And it was her way of bringing up the exception that I could not easily excuse. In a moment of reverse logic this woman equated adoption with being different . . . the necessary ingredient for a creative writing career. Ergo, my adoption was the one and only thing that made me different.

If she had left it at that, if she had said, "You could be a writer because you're different, even if you were only adopted," then I could almost have understood how she managed to get from point "A" to point "B." But she added an element of insult to injury when she carried her misguided notion a step further by claiming that it was only my "difference," my adoption, that I would be able to write about, and nothing more.

Could I have been over-reacting to her innocuous remarks? Possibly. But I don't think I was. I think I had a pretty good handle on what she was saying and what she wasn't saying. Whether or not she thought I had any literary potential was not the issue. I knew she didn't know what she was talking about. Yet, somehow her remarks about my adoption got to me. After all the years I had known this woman, I was surprised she had such antediluvian notions about adoption and adoptees.

I only wish I had had the nerve to challenge her, to ask her what it was about adoption that made me different. Unfortunately, or fortunately, depending on how you view respect for your elders, I didn't make an issue of the issue. Nothing would have been gained by a confrontation, so I decided to depart with my integrity intact.

There was a moral in that visitation of twenty years ago, one that helped me reshape my new-found idealism. I learned that the courage of one's conviction had to be deeply rooted in a strong sense of self.

If I wanted to continue to grow, if I wanted to take my year's experience abroad and make it the focal point of my redirected life, I was going to have to develop a much thicker skin and be prepared for many more negative assaults on my idealistic world-view.

It was all a part of my coming of age. It was one more transition I was making. And to make the most of that transition time, I had to hold my ground. As anyone who came of age during the late 1960's and early 1970's knows, holding one's ground was not an easy task, considering the political and social climate of the age.

My last year in college coincided with the decline of the American dream. We were fighting a very unpopular war in Vietnam. The youth of America was divided by diametrically opposed allegiances. Prophets of doom were at their zenith. And then there was me. I was filled with optimism. I saw evolution where others saw revolution as the only way out. Instead of engaging in anti-war demonstrations or pro-war marches, I was actively involved in Marist College's Children's Theatre, rehearsing for a production of *The Wizard of Oz*.

On a worldwide scale, my role as the Tinman in a minor production of a children's classic was not about to tip the scale in either direction, but again, it made a lasting impression on me. I had always viewed the story of Dorothy as nothing more than just a great children's book that eventually gave Judy Garland one of the plum movie roles in her career.

As a child I had read Frank L. Baum's novel two or three times, and I had seen the movie at least a half-dozen times before getting a role in my college production of the story. As a child I had identified with Dorothy Gale. It wasn't until I studied the story in earnest, though, that I felt such empathy for her. She too was an adoptee. We never learn what happened to her parents, but we do know she was raised by her Aunt Em and Uncle Henry. We never learn if they were her blood-relatives, or whether "aunt" and "uncle" were merely Dorothy's courtesy titles for them. In any case, Dorothy was not raised by her birth parents.

She was treated well, although she wasn't really understood by her relatives and the farmhands. She dreamed of a place that was "over the rainbow," a place where dreams come true, a place where she would eventually find the yellow brick road.

As a character in the play, I traveled with Dorothy during many a rehearsal and quite a few performances. I'll never forget how confused I was by Frank L. Baum's ending, when the Good Witch gives Dorothy's traveling companions the things they had sought—a brain, a heart, and courage. After telling Dorothy she has always had the power to return home to Kansas, the Good Witch Glinda asks her what she has learned in Oz.

"I learned," Dorothy tells Glinda, "that if you go looking for your heart's desire and can't find it in your own backyard, you never really lost it in the first place."

How I used to hate that line every time it was spoken. I didn't believe a word of it. If you couldn't find happiness in your own backyard, you were obligated to go looking for it, no matter where your search took you. I was a self-proclaimed seeker. I had left my own backyard to find a greater measure of happiness, and I had found it.

That part was true. I had found a new source of happiness, but I hadn't found it in Oxford, and I hadn't found it in any of the books I had read.

As much as I hated to admit it, Dorothy was right. Unless you found happiness in your own backyard— and by that, I think Baum meant within yourself—you'd never really find it.

Searching is not something you have to run off to the far corners of the world to accomplish. A contemplative monk, who might never wander away from the monastery grounds, can achieve the same level of understanding and awareness as can a person who spends a lifetime traveling the seven seas in pursuit of heightened awareness. What matters is that, as a result of the search, the individual arrives at the center of his or her being.

My mother never traveled the world. She never read the great philosophical books, but she did arrive at the center, because she looked in her own backyard.

It wasn't until I understood the real meaning of Dorothy's reply that I was at all prepared to embark on an adoption search. If I had begun that search any earlier, I would have been searching in vain because the real search, the one I had to embark on first, was the search for myself.

Baum's philosophy as expressed in *The Wizard of Oz* might appear to be childlike and innocent . . . and therefore not worthy of any adult consideration . . . but the meaning of his message is universal. Unfortunately, as we grow older, we often lose the vision of innocence and begin to view things with skepticism. We forget the message expressed in another children's classic, *The Little Prince*, that "it is only with the heart that one sees rightly. What is essential is invisible to the eye."

Whether I had not matured enough to become skeptical is a matter for debate. I only know that I looked for the same honesty and ring of truth in all the writers I read. And I found it in several places. I found it when I first read T. S. Eliot at Oxford. I can honestly say that for the first time in my life I truly understood the central message of our earthly existence when I read "East Coker" in Eliot's *The Four Quartets*.

Everything seemed to come together when I found that poem, because my thoughts and feelings were put into words by the poet, and I didn't feel alone anymore.

I knew that the road to truth and understanding was not an easy road. In "East Coker" Eliot proclaimed that life was a journey that demanded a certain amount of detachment from self and the distractions of the world. It was a journey that required the traveler to focus on a goal that could only be achieved through a personal transformation.

Of course, Eliot was not the first to discover the path to understanding. The message in "East Coker" could be found also in the teachings of Christ, Buddha, and Mohammed. Lessons that could be learned in the Bible and the Koran and the Talmud have long been at our disposal. Why we have not been quick to say "yes" to them remains only a partial mystery. It's not hard to understand that a message that espouses a way of ingenuousness, dispossession, and a certain degree of suffering would not be unanimously adopted by people who seek pleasure and comfort. Comfort and pleasure, however, are more often than not obstacles to real happiness. No matter how Oz might sparkle in the distance, no matter how brilliant the yellow brick road, the path of least resistance is not the path to take.

This is something I secretly knew before I embarked on my adoption search. I knew I was not going to arrive at nirvana when my search came to an end. My adoption search was part of my life search. Taken out of context, my search would have been nothing more than an ego trip. Taken in the context of my personal growth and development, my search for my missing links was a step in the right direction on the road less traveled.

Even as I write these words, I'm still involved in my search. I can only hope that my seeking will never end. I can only hope that my eyes will stay open to new and wonderful things. I can only hope that the winds of destiny will continue to catch my sails and keep me seeking wherever they drive my boat.

CHAPTER FIFTEEN

Loose Ends

BY THE TIME you've reached the end of a novel, when the curtain comes down on the last act of a play, or when the credits begin rolling after the final scene in a movie, usually most, if not all, the loose ends have been neatly tied up. If a murder has been committed, you know who did it. If a marriage has been in trouble, you either close the book or leave the theater knowing what is going to happen.

Art is like that. The author has ultimate control over the ending of his or her work. If the writer intentionally leaves you hanging, it isn't until he or she has at least offered some resolutions to the conflict introduced in the story.

Life never seems to allow for such neat and tidy endings. No sooner has one chapter come to a close than another one begins. And then another. Such was the case when I began the search for my missing links. And such was the case when I began writing the account of my search. It always seemed that when I was about to close in on a new discovery, another new twist developed. And with each twist, the focus of my story took a slightly different direction.

I may have reached the final lap of my search, but the finish line is still ahead of me, and it will always be slightly out of reach, because there are still some loose ends to be tied. As satisfied as I am with what I have learned and the many new family members I have met, I have this empty feeling, because my half-brother's story has been left hanging. It's very fortunate my half-brother has such an understanding nature, or he would not be so willing to comply with my birth mother's wish that he not make contact with her. He understands the sensitivity of the situation, although that doesn't make it any easier for him. He'd very much like to meet his birth mother. He'd like to reach out to her and tell her that it's all right. He'd like to tell her that whatever happened, happened a long time ago when he was only an innocent player in her tragic story.

I did my best to remove the barriers of ignorance at Christmas 1987 when I finally worked up the courage to tell my birth mother that I had located her other son. I had to tell her. I couldn't live with myself knowing that I was holding back a key piece of information that had to do with her life. I owed it to my birth mother to be honest with her. I owed it to my half-brother to pave the way for what we both hope will be an eventual reunion.

My half-brother and I have even imagined the way it will happen. We'll be appearing on *The Donahue Show* with other adoptees. The theme might be adoptees who were fathered by Catholic priests. Phil will mention to the audience that my half-brother has not yet met his birth mother. But, he'll add, that is all about to change. And with that our birth mother will walk on stage. That's what I'd like to see happen. If not on *The Donahue Show*, then at my house or my half-brother's home.

I'd also like to tie the other loose end in my sibling story. I'd like to resolve the mystery and identity of my

other sibling. And even though I understand that re-
solving that part of my search might take years, I believe someday I'll be able to write the final chapter of
that part of my search. That chapter might neatly sum
up my search, but I still wouldn't be completely satisfied, because my sister's search has moved very little
since my own began.

All my sister Patti knows about her birth parents
comes from the non-identifying information she received from The Foundling Home. She was born Patricia Janice Dowden on July 11, 1946 at St. Vincent's Hospital in New York City. Her birth mother was 24 years
old and single at the time. Her birth father was 23 and
married. Both were, or had recently been, in the armed
services. He never knew he had fathered a child, because Patti's birth mother never told him.

Patti also learned that her birth mother was one of
three daughters in a Protestant family. Her maternal
grandfather was 54 years of age and her grandmother
was 52 when Patti was born.

That's the sum total of what she knows. She can't
get any further information from the Foundling. The
hospital won't give her access to any records. And
whenever she applies for a copy of her original birth certificate, she is sent a copy amended by adoption. The
only real thing she has to go on is the name "Dowden,"
but in all adoptee stories there is the nagging doubt that
the surname given by the mother may have been a red
herring—a name made up at the time of the child's
birth. The name may have no connection with the real
identity of the adoptee. And even if Dowden was Patti's
real name, there's no way of knowing where her birth
mother's home was then . . . or is now.

I should know the difficulty of tracing a parent named Dowden, because I spent time searching through old New York City directories looking for individuals named Dowden. Unfortunately, my search didn't turn up a solid lead. And I wasn't surprised. Both my sister and I are convinced that her birth mother was only in New York to deliver her baby. We imagine that she got pregnant while she was still in the service, but more than likely was out of the service before the Army or Navy knew about her condition. Or maybe they did know and required her to leave the service. That's the problem with adoption searches: you never can have enough information.

But, that doesn't mean I'm giving up on my sister's search. I haven't begun to exhaust all the possibilities. And who knows, a copy of this book might fall into the right hands. The next thing you know, my sister will be joining my half-brother and me on *The Donahue Show*. The theme would be different, no longer about priests' children, but maybe just about adoptee searches.

It could happen, but not before I follow up on another part of the mission I've set myself, the search for my late Aunt Arlene's two children. Joan has told me that her sister had always wanted to find her children but thought it was impossible . . . until I found my birth mother. That rekindled her hope. Unfortunately, her untimely death put an end to the possibility of her realizing her dream. That doesn't mean, however, that her life or search were in vain. I'd like to be able to find her two children—my cousins—if only to tell them that their birth mother loved them. And—you guessed it—I'd like to share the stage with them on *The Donahue Show*.

Tying up those loose ends would be very satisfying, but it still wouldn't be the end to all the loose ends. There are still the many unanswered questions about my birth father. I still have hope that I'll eventually be able to meet my birth father's sister. It might not happen next week, next month, or next year, but I believe, or I want to believe it *will* happen. (On *The Donahue Show?*)

On a more philosophical note, I'm still at loose ends about pregnancy and the priesthood. On the one hand, I am resolute in my belief that priests, in the priesthood as it is now, should not become biological fathers. On the other hand, however, I don't think the Church should be so resolute in its opposition to married clergy. I've studied the New Testament, and I've combed through enough theological books and magazines, and I'm still not convinced the Church's stand on celibacy has any real religious validity.

A rule is a rule, however, and if you don't like the rules, you don't play the game. But, if you believe in the game enough, and you want to play in it, you work toward changing the rules, not breaking them.

I might want to believe my birth father had a right to exercise his human sexuality, but not at the expense of his vows. As hard as it is for me to admit it, my birth father broke the rules for his own personal convenience, not because he was a pioneer in advancing priests' rights. My birth father was a man of the cloth with a weakness of the flesh. It would have been better if he had learned from his weakness, but it's obvious that he went to bat at least twice and scored both times. Whether or not he ever scored again is something I might never know. But what I do know is this: my birth father was not alone in losing his battle against the temptation of the flesh. I have another half-brother who is evidence of that. And I don't believe my half-brothers and I are the only exceptions to the rule. That statement is not offered as an excuse for priests who succumb to sexual desires, but rather as a fact that has been ignored for too long.

I wish I had a definitive answer to this thorny question. I don't. I only know that the problem of diminishing vocations will create an expanding crisis until the Church recognizes the need to re-evaluate its long-standing position on celibacy. Not that I think the concept of celibacy should be abandoned altogether. I do think, however, that a man . . . and a woman . . . should be able to choose a priestly life either celibate or in the married state. I know if I had the option . . . today . . . I would seriously consider the priesthood . . . as a married man. (Sort of "like father, like son.")

That about sums up my loose ends, with one small exception. I'm still not satisfied with the adoptee's plight. There are too many millions of adoptees of all ages with a myriad of needs and unanswered questions. I would like to see some of the "cloak and dagger" put to rest. I would like to see more attention paid to the fine work being done by many adoptee rights groups. I would like to see more understanding on the part of the non-adoptees of the world. I would also like to see society take a healthier stand on what it means to be a mother or a father.

I worry that we live in a society that not only condones, but also advocates, single motherhood. Not that I want to bring back the dark ages, but I do believe that a child should have the benefit of a mother and a father.

Divorce has resulted in far too many broken families as it is, leaving many children in single-parent homes. And while I would agree that it's far better to come from a broken home than to live in a breaking home, I can't bring myself to advocate deliberate single-parent families, unless it's a case of a man or woman adopting a child who otherwise would have no parent at all.

I firmly believe in women's rights, but I wonder if those rights extend to childbearing without the benefit of a father to participate in raising his child.

I'm well aware that this last loose end of mine opens up another Pandora's box the contents of which touch upon everything from surrogate motherhood to *in vitro* fertilization, but I wonder if the powers that be have stopped to think of the next generation of children who, not born of a mother and father in the traditional way, may embark on a search for their missing links.

How hard, I think, if not impossible, it will be for the child born of artificial insemination to locate his or her birth father. Will such a child be satisfied to know that that birth father was a Petri dish? Won't the child want to know more about him . . . the man? Won't he or she want to know from whom his or her long fingers, blond hair, artistic abilities came? Won't he or she want to know whether the families of the previous generation hailed from Germany or Italy?

I wonder. I wonder a lot about things that sometimes don't seem really to matter to many people. But most of all, I wonder if we'll forget how to wonder. I worry that we'll forget how to lift the sails and catch the winds of destiny in search of meaning. Because life without meaning is a life of restlessness and vague desires. It is a boat longing for the sea . . . and yet afraid.

About the Author

Vincent J. Begley combines writing and marketing careers in New York City, where his interest in the theater has led to his participation in numerous theatrical and TV productions. A graduate of Marist College in Poughkeepsie, New York, he also completed advanced graduate studies in writing at Manchester College, Oxford.

He and his wife Patty and their four children live in Chester, New York.

About the Book

Missing Links was typeset in Palacio on Compugraphic MCS by Margaret Buckley. The book was printed and bound by McNaughton & Gunn, Inc. of Ann Arbor, MI. Text paper is acid-free Glatfelter Natural.